HOLDING THE ROPE

HOLDING THE ROPE

SHORT-TERM MISSIONS, LONG-TERM IMPACT

CLINT ARCHER

WILLIAM CAREY
LIBRARY

Published by William Carey Library
1605 E. Elizabeth Street
Pasadena, CA 91104 | www.missionbooks.org

Melissa Hicks, editor
Brad Koenig, copyeditor
Hugh Pindur, graphic designer   ·
Rose Lee-Norman, indexer

William Carey Library is a ministry of the
U.S. Center for World Mission
Pasadena, CA | www.uscwm.org

Printed in the United States of America
18 17 16 15 14   5 4 3 2 1 BP300

Library of Congress Cataloging-in-Publication Data

Archer, Clint.
  Holding the rope : short-term missions, long-term impact / by Clint Archer.
    pages cm
  ISBN 978-0-87808-628-3
  1. Short-term missions. I. Title.
  BV2082.S56A73 2014
  266--dc23
                          2014000601

To **Rick Holland**
who taught me how to hold the rope,
and to **Joel James**
who showed how to dangle joyfully from the other end.

CONTENTS

FOREWORD

Not long ago I read a missions article on why churches should cancel their short-term missions (STM) program. At great length, the author graphically detailed the *faux pas* of well-meaning Westerners, recounting how houses got painted multiple times or churches and orphanages were built but never used—all in the name of short term missions. His remedy? Just send money, not people. After all, stewardship suggests that locals can do the job for a fraction of the cost!

While the author's caricature may have been deliberately exaggerated, he did have a point. Sometimes work can be done more reasonably with local help. Some projects undoubtedly are created simply to keep unsolicited STM volunteers busy. But one must be careful not to throw out the proverbial baby with the bath water. Just because an instrument is misused doesn't mean one discards it altogether.

Ultimately, the issue is not about painting houses, erecting buildings, or sending financial resources. Rather, it all boils down to what the greatest manual on missions says about STM's.

Did the greatest short-term missionary ever send his disciples on an STM? Is there biblical precedent for STM's? Does the Great Commission (Matt 28:18–20) endorse STM endeavors?

Clint Archer answers these questions with a resounding, "Absolutely Yes!" The greatest short-term missionary himself sent his disciples on an STM (Matt 10:1–15; Luke 9:1–6). The Holy Spirit sent Barnabas and Saul on an STM (Acts 13). The apostle Paul was ministered to by Timothy and Epaphroditus, an STM team (Phil 2:19–28), and John Mark (2 Tim 4:11). Through these texts and others, Archer argues convincingly that the validity of any STM trip and its on-field activity must be determined by its conformity to the principles of God's Word and driven by its commitment to following the biblical protocols.

Building off the famous quote of William Carey, Archer argues that STM's are designed to "hold the ropes" for long-term missionaries. In doing so, he underscores the fact that truly biblical ministry is not a solo sport, that even long-term "lone rangers" need someone to help. Short-term versus long-term need not nor should not be an either-or proposition. STM activity is a support network to long-term missionaries, a "side dish to complement that meal; it isn't the whole menu" (23). Later, Archer adds, "STM takes the soothing balm of fellowship and encouragement to our missionaries. Our missionaries are our mission!" (33).

While an STM team may be given opportunities for evangelism, discipleship, and teaching, these opportunities, carried out at the request of the missionary, are nonetheless examples of "holding the rope." Long-term soldiers know the lay of the land; STM recruits are there to help them carry out their biblical mandates, to serve them in whatever manner deemed most beneficial to the missionary.

The issue facing STM's is not whether they are right or wrong. Yes, invading some foreign battleground wrongly motivated, ill-prepared, and uninvited is wrong. It is a recipe for disaster. But canceling them altogether could be one of the greatest travesties to the missionary endeavors of the twenty-first century!

That is why I am particularly thankful for this in-depth treatment of short-term missions by Clint Archer. Built on a thoroughly biblical foundation, it lays out the framework for avoiding the criticisms and pitfalls of misled short-term, cross-cultural ministries. It is a wonderful guidebook for pastors, missions-minded laypeople and, yes, even mission executives. It is a crucial reminder to keep the focus in every mission endeavor in its rightful place, at the forefront of the local church's commitment to the Great Commission. And, keeping its foundation biblical will infuse your church with enthusiasm for spreading the Good News and will promote worship and praise to the One who builds his church.

STM can be and should be a key component of every church's mission. Because, as Archer concludes: "Holding the ropes is no less vital to the success of the mission than it is to penetrate the dark pit" (111).

Irv Busenitz, ThD

academic dean and vice president of The Master's Seminary

chairman of the board of Elder's Council Handling Outreach (ECHO)

at Grace Community Church

INTRODUCTION:
A LEGACY OF HOLDING THE ROPE

"Expect great things of God. Attempt great things for God." These immortal words of missionary pioneer William Carey became the manifesto of the modern missionary endeavor. This diametric pair of imperatives formed the simple outline of a sermon Carey preached to a generation of churchmen who had been simmering in apathy toward foreign missions. And how charming that one who mended shoes for a living would be used by God to address the church's state of spiritual disrepair. His pair of points was profound in their simplicity. This quaint coincidence was not lost on his eminent biographer (and descendant) Pearce Carey, who wrote eloquently of the so-called "deathless sermon":

> For seventeen years he had been making things in his workshop
> in pairs, and this sermon fell under the unconscious power of the
> same habit. His pair of "biddings"—the right- and left-foot shoes
> for every pilgrim and soldier of the Lord—rang with homely brev-
> ity and unorthodox audacity. By contrast with the multi-headed,
> many-jointed sermons of the period (and in particular Association
> sermons) he dared to be simple and direct. His words were not for
> display but for persuasion; not to secure personal pulpit success,
> but to win a case, a very battle for his Lord.[1]

---

1   S. Pearce Carey, *William Carey* (London: Wakeman Trust, 1993), 77.

The effect of the incisive sermon was immediately palpable. One awestruck member of the audience, John Ryland, who days later would chair the very meeting that begot the world's first Baptist foreign missionary society, said, "Had all the people lifted up their voice and wept, as the children of Israel did at Bochim, I should not have wondered, so clearly did he prove the *criminality* of our supineness in the cause of God.[2]

Like Paul going to the Gentiles, Carey burned with passion for what he called "the heathen." He was dissatisfied with the humdrum notion of only safely sharing the gospel among compatriots, ensconced in the comfort and security of home. He boiled with a deeper longing, to escape the trappings of familiarity and venture into the uncertain and uncharted spiritual territory haunted by paganism and superstition. And his passion was infectious.

It was the same week that he preached that sermon that the fraternity of regional pastors met to make history. The little conclave of inauspicious ministers was in that moment the first Baptist missions board in the world.

When the time came to initiate the mission, the band of brothers had the money (or so they thought; the estimates they were given were woefully inaccurate). They had a providentially chosen field: India. They knew their mandate: reach the teeming masses of heathen Hindus resident in Asia with the gospel of salvation in Jesus Christ alone. They clung to the imprimatur of God's promise to bless the spread of his word (Isa 55:10,11). And they even had a relatively clear methodology—namely, to deploy a volunteer to learn the language, translate the Scriptures, and disseminate the gospel. There was only one quintessential element of success missing—a missionary.

The man who had brought them the opportunity had laid the foundation for India, but lacked the linguistic skill needed for the most pressing work of translation. The committee needed a man who had the spiritual fortitude to be a witness for Christ in a dark place, the physical mettle to endure an inclement climate, the linguistic acumen to rapidly learn a completely unknown tongue, the theological and linguistic credentials up to the task of translating Greek and Hebrew, and the doughtiness of character to hack living away from home.

---

2   Ibid., 76.

It soon became apparent that the short list of candidates was conveniently very short. It consisted of only one name, that of the polyglot cobbler, William Carey.

No one who knew the thirty-one-year-old Carey would hesitate to propose his candidacy. He was a cobbler by trade, but a statesman at heart. His prescience of this moment was well known. He had been preparing for this class of service his whole life. He had a prodigious linguistic ability, which was discovered when he learned Latin from his father with astonishing facility at age five. And although his formal academic training was not impressive on paper, his heuristic efforts were legendary. The cobbler's obscure English workshop hosted an academy of self-learning, and while his hands were occupied with tapping and stitching, his mind was preoccupied with parsing and conjugating. Carey employed this gift of languages like a wise steward, beavering away at teaching himself Greek, Hebrew, Italian, Dutch, and French. He also immersed himself in theology and biblical studies while teaching school and pastoring a church. This was a man who knew how to work and study, and he was renowned for his passionate desire to reach foreign people groups who were lost without Christ.

Only one question remained: would he be willing?

Carey had set his heart on the lost souls of Tahiti. India was decidedly less attractive, geographically speaking. It is a testimony of his selfless sincerity that the shift in direction brought no pause to his commitment. But the prospect of an isolated pioneer work in the mysterious land of India would be daunting to even the most intrepid soul. Carey's declaration of intent was tempered with the realization that he would need help. He would need financial, logistic, emotional, and spiritual support. He knew this work needed to be done, and felt he could do it if he knew there was someone back home connected to him and his cause. In an historic committee meeting, late on the night of January 10, 1793, Carey's colleague Andrew Fuller commented that India was a gold mine of lost souls, and asked, "Who will venture to explore it?" Carey declared his willingness to accept the challenge with the immortal words that would echo for centuries as a motto for countless future missionaries: "I will go down, but remember that you must hold the ropes."[3]

---

3   John Belcher, *William Carey: A Biography* (Philadelphia: American Baptist Publication Society, 1853), 73–74.

And with that he earned the moniker, the father of modern missions. The acceptance of a commission to translocate abroad permanently for the sole reason of propagating the gospel internationally, relying on a support infrastructure from home, was a new and trailblazing system that would prove one of the most effective ways to accomplish the Great Commission. And at its core is the commitment of the senders to the goers to firmly hold the ropes of support.

"Holding the ropes" is more than a catchphrase. It articulates the epitome of an entire philosophy of ministry. Christian missions is too daunting an enterprise to attempt alone. Christians are not spiritual hermits. God knits us together in a body, and each member is reliant on the others. We are an interconnected web of relationships and resources, and together the synergy of our combined efforts can accomplish untold advancement for the kingdom of God.

The home-based support of the full-time satellite missionary is the way most Christians will respond to the injunction of our Lord to reach the world. Iconic missionary Hudson Taylor once said, "Missions is not an option to be considered, it is a command to be obeyed."

The challenge that faces us is to consider not what the bare minimum requirement is for a church to be obedient to the Great Commission, but what *more* can be done with what we have been given? William Carey turned the tide of history with a simple, pleading question he posed to Andrew Fuller, his like-minded friend and fellow member of the Baptist fraternity of ministers who met at Nottingham in 1792. It was the meeting at which Carey had preached his renowned "deathless sermon" that challenged the ministers to "expect great things of God, attempt great things for God." The seventeen delegates were about to close the business of the day without any resolution in favor of initiating a mission to the lost. This would be the second time Carey was disappointed. Carey turned in desperation to Fuller, grasped his arm, and cried out, "Is there nothing again going to be done, sir?" That simple, pointed question broke through the barricade of Fuller's ambivalence.

In the inimitable words of Pearce Carey:

This proved a creative moment in the history of evangelistic endeavor. Deep called unto deep. Fuller trembled an instant under
that desperate, heart-broken gesture, and then his own soul was
stabbed awake, and the Holy Ghost flooded his spirit. He also heard
God's sigh at the need of the lost. Often he had sympathized with
Carey's propaganda, though too timorous for committal. Now, in
a moment, he became convert and colleague, the first of Carey's
captives, the first of Christ's "expectant attempters."[4]

Fuller's alliance was the catalyst that galvanized the support of the
rest of the group, and their respective churches, and eventually the entire
denomination. The committee reconvened its discussion and didn't close
business until they passed Carey's motion to resolve a plan to form a "Particular
Baptist Society for propagating the Gospel among the Heathen." The rest is,
as we say, history.

———

As the world turns, people scurry like ants to build their respective
fiefdoms of influence. Companies merge and grow, populations explode and
expand, empires conquer and reclaim, and societies upgrade and increase in
the interminable pursuit of betterment. And all the while the real kingdom
growth is happening silently but surely in the spiritual realm. We call it
missions.

- "Your kingdom come, your will be done, on earth as it is in
  heaven." (Matt 6:10)
- "And Jesus came and said to them, 'All authority in heaven and
  on earth has been given to me. Go therefore and make disciples
  of all nations, baptizing them in the name of the Father and of
  the Son and of the Holy Spirit, teaching them to observe all that

---

4   S. Pearce Carey, *William Carey*, 78.

I have commanded you. And behold, I am with you always, to the end of the age.'" (Matt 28:18–20)

- "Being asked by the Pharisees when the kingdom of God would come, he answered them, 'The kingdom of God is not coming in ways that can be observed, nor will they say, "Look, here it is!" or "There!" for behold, the kingdom of God is in the midst of you.'" (Luke 17:20,21)
- "For we do not wrestle against flesh and blood, but against the rulers, against the authorities, against the cosmic powers over this present darkness, against the spiritual forces of evil in the heavenly places." (Eph 6:12)

Missions is nothing less than an organized, revolutionary assault on the unseen forces of the present darkness by a spiritual legion of soldiers who fight for the extension of God's kingdom to dominate the universe. And local churches are the bastions that defend that cause, forge the weapons, train the soldiers, and populate the ranks with men and women bent on spreading God's fame or dying as they try.

That is Carey's legacy. And he merely accepted the torch that was lit by the Apostle Paul, who in turn was simply following the marching orders of his King Jesus.

When Paul was commissioned to take the gospel to the Gentiles, his journeys blazed the trail for those who would emulate his example in the future, those who eschew the sedentary life in favor of a mobile mission. All Christians have a compulsion to spread God's glory and the good news of salvation in Jesus. But some have a deeper urge driving them, the craving to *go*.

Thank God that there are still men and women who hear the clarion call of God to storm the gates of hell on foreign soil. And thank God for the many supporters who make the campaign possible by holding the ropes.

This book is an attempt to help the helpers. Short-term missions is an essential part of supporting the missionaries we send. The following chapters will hopefully help shape your understanding of and appreciation for the vital role short-term teams play in undergirding the work missionaries do.

1

SHORT-TERM TRIP, LONG-TERM DAMAGE

I felt called to Botswana. Actually I felt called to date this girl, and she was going to Botswana, so for me the call was just as clear. I was a freshman in college, a spiritual neophyte whose theology was limited to Christianese sound bites (justification is living "just as if I" hadn't sinned; atonement is the "at-one-ment" of man and God). This opportunity was for an all-expenses-paid trip—thanks to the widow's mites and other donations. Ten days of roughing it in Africa, including four days of overland travel in 4x4 Land Rovers. It was a Camel adventure for nonsmokers, a way to beef up my passport stamp collection, and a chance to serve God under the gaze of the girl I liked. I was sold. So, armed with four hours of training and the Roman's Road freshly memorized, I overpacked my knapsack and joined the band of brothers and sisters who would take the gospel to the unreached masses in the Kalahari desert. Whoever said being a Christian wasn't fun?

KALAHARI CONUNDRUMS

The adventure was not exactly the way I had pictured it. Four dusty days in a Jeep seems a less glamorous journey now that I've experienced it. Since none of the vehicles had air conditioning, I selfishly opted for the convertible. I soon discovered that the most underappreciated tool on my Swiss Army knife, which I affectionately dubbed "MacGyver," is the toothpick. I frequently employed it to exorcise from my teeth the legion of tiny bugs that lodged there as we zipped through the dunes like a brood of determined sidewinders. Incidentally, the journey home in the closed-roof vehicle was just as grueling. Frying in a steel box on wheels is only marginally less torturous than being force fed with fauna all day long.

The six days that we were with the missionaries were even more challenging to my city-slicker constitution. Water took forty minutes to pump manually and transport back to the compound. We bathed in a steel drum, the entire grimy team reusing the same water. During the day under the blazing sun we dug and hoisted, mixed and measured, in order to erect a corrugated-tin-roof shelter that would function as a gathering place for the six or seven local believers who met weekly with the missionaries. In our prayer letters we labeled that project "building a church," but it was so shoddy that I suspect it cost the missionary some personal funds after we left to tear it down and have it rebuilt in a way that didn't unnecessarily jeopardize the lives of his little flock.

The team members were not the only disillusioned foreigners. The missionary family's workload multiplied exponentially for the duration of our stay. They labored to cook for us, transport us, train and retrain us, and constantly did damage control with the locals as we committed one cultural *faux pas* after another. (I feel it should be noted that I was not one of those who giggled at the sight of the bare-breasted deaconess we met, though I was the only one who couldn't stomach the meal we were served that night, for which I blame the bug blitz for my loss of appetite.)

The highlight for me was preaching the gospel to an attentive native tribe through a translator. I walked them passionately through the colors of the beaded bracelet we awarded to anyone who said they believed. Not surprisingly we made many "converts" that day. The exotic plastic beads were apparently worth changing religion for. The missionary wisely suggested that baptisms were only performed after a follow-up visit he would make the following week; i.e., when we were out of the way.

The lowlight was when I crawled into my tent in the midmorning to get more sunblock for me and the team who were cementing poles into the ground for the church we were constructing. Exhausted, I decided to put my head to the pillow for a mere minute of respite from the labor. I awoke four hours later facing the bitter glares of the rest of the team and, most significantly, the girl I had been trying to impress. I let down the team, the girl, the missionaries, and—I'm forgetting someone—oh yes, God.

The trip was undeniably a PowerPoint success story. We had secured a cornucopia of colorful photos with pithy captions to document our accomplishments. A tribe had heard the gospel, my preaching ability had been affirmed, and we delivered a sterling report to our supporters back home who had all been holding vigil, waiting for the bottom line: how many souls from Botswana will be in heaven because of our cash?

Sadly, I never heard from anyone in the team again. We were not from the same church, and so we moved in different ecclesiastical circles. And the missionaries never heard from me. I cannot for the life of me remember their names, or how many kids they had. But I do remember feeling sorry for them that they had to bathe in that steel drum, and because they had no friends.

MORE HARM THAN GOOD?

I couldn't help feeling that we had got more out of the trip than the missionaries. We had been a burden on them. We didn't leave them with any tangible benefit (that church roof was a real hazard to the community). We didn't foster deep relationships with them. And there was no talk of the team going back, or of personally becoming supporters of their ministry financially.

I think we might actually have done some long-term damage. We left a few natives thinking they were saved because they nodded at the right time and were issued with a colored bracelet, which for all I know became another idol in their pantheon. I learned later that a diamond mining corporation regularly delivered food supplies and alcohol to the tribe in exchange for them peacefully relocating and staying off the land that rightfully belonged to them. This crippled their society by removing any incentive to work. The problem was compounded when eager, white college students showed up and erected buildings, did manual labor, and then disappeared, leaving gifts and supplies behind for the missionaries. Just like the diamond mine representatives. The missionaries struggled to set an example that hard work was a virtue. This effort was subverted by teams like ours.

I was plagued by the question, why would the missionary even consent to a team, let alone request one? In later years I discovered how missionaries are often forced to work the system in order to get ministry done. For example, let us say the missionary needs $5,000 to complete a church building. This money will go to hiring local labor, paying them generously and providing incentive for them to work. It will create a community project where natives will work side by side with the missionaries, where they will develop relationships, camaraderie, and a sense of accomplishment. There is no time limit to the project, so the missionary can use the time to teach the men how to lay foundations, mix cement, and other skills that they could use to improve their own community. He can also interrupt work to tend to other needs in the community or to discuss spiritual matters with his building crew. What the missionary needs is cash, and perhaps a skilled builder to help train the locals. What he doesn't need is ten college students who take a week off between their accounting classes to crank out a project they have no experience in, divorced from the local community, and leaving nothing but a rushed structure that the locals view as yet another foreign intrusion into their community.

But if the missionary requests $5,000 cash for a building project, they will be denied. "Funds are scarce, and you already get a fixed amount of support. We want to bring on more missionaries so we can have more flags on the world map at our mission display table." And yet if the missionary shrewdly requests a Short-term Missions (STM) team to do the project, the church leaps into the excited enthusiastic support of a trip that will cost potentially ten times as much if airfare is needed. But this is in line with their image as a missions-minded church, so the fund-raising machine kicks in and pops out another ineffective STM team.

I didn't realize all this at the time. But after my return from Botswana I knew there had to be a better way to do STM trips than this. I stopped short of making a rash vow to never go on another STM trip, but I learned enough about myself and about STM that I knew I would think long and hard before signing up for another one. It would have to be a very profitable trip, and have someone very special, for me to consider another foray into the Kalahari, or anywhere they didn't have hot water.

THE GHOST OF STM PAST

Fast-forward four years. I had matured somewhat, learned the real definition of justification and other cool words like infralapsarianism. I did date that girl, but we parted ways through a series of increasingly messy breakups (that had nothing to do with STM, but a little to do with my irresponsibility evidenced by things like naps I took at times I should be working), culminating in me moving overseas to go to seminary. It was in seminary that I was confronted with STM again, in a most unlikely and providential way.

I was serving in the college ministry of a ten-thousand-member church. They had a vast STM program, which I knew nothing about and had no interest in, until one fateful day. Although the church supported over sixty missionary families and sent out about twelve trips a year, there was only one part-time intern who ran STM single-handedly. In an attempt to help this overworked fellow survive, the church created a position one rung below intern. On a literal ladder this rung is actually the ground. What job is below an intern that is paid next to nothing? I think people call it a "gopher" (go for this, go for that), errand boy, or lackey. The church, in an attempt at instilling dignity in the job title, called it "Volunteer Assistant to the STM Coordinator." The job came with no business cards, and no pay, but it did come with a spot on an STM team, fully supported by the church.

As a dirt-poor international student, a free trip home to visit family and friends seemed like a gift from God I couldn't ignore. Before I knew what happened, I raised my hand and signed up for a year of work in exchange for a plane ticket and a three-week trip to South Africa with two friends who were considering permanent ministry there, and with a fiancée. I was now engaged to a godly, beautiful American girl who committed to saying yes to the proposal without even seeing my home country. I figured this would be a good opportunity for her to discover what she had got herself into. Her host home while in-country was my parents' house. Since we weren't married, my host home was at another location, which in a bizarre irony was the same house that the girl from the Botswana trip had lived in the whole time I knew her. I'm not sure what the significance is, but I always said if I wrote a book, I'd drop that detail in there. Meanwhile, my fiancée was thrown in the deep end getting to know my "interesting" family, without me around. I hadn't thought this through. But she was committed enough that it didn't do any permanent damage to our relationship.

This trip was just as useless as my previous experience, but this time I didn't care. I got to visit home for three weeks and hang out with my friends and family, only occasionally interrupted with ministry responsibilities. And it was all for free. Then it happened.

INTERVIEW WITH A VAMPIRE

Remember that I was dirt poor, only now I was engaged. My visa limited me to working part time, and on campus. So I quickly climbed the seminary corporate ladder from janitorial staff to bookshop (better pay) to library (better hours). The seminary was on the same campus as the megachurch I was attending, so a job at the church was a legal loophole a small number of fortunate international seminary students managed to crawl through. The church had very few jobs for seminoids, but they were generally internships that involved paying for tuition, free coffee in the break room, and less work that involved heavy boxes that made me want to nap after a shift when I should be learning Greek or something.

One day I was lugging boxes of books that felt like they were lined with lead. I was dressed in shorts and a sweaty T-shirt. I got a call from the church outreach department. I jogged up to the church office, affectionately called "the kingdom hall" by us plebs who worked in the basement of the library. I was pretty sure the call had something to do with moving a heavy box, something the delicate interns usually staffed out to us blue-collar types. But this meeting was about something totally unexpected.

The receptionist buzzed me through the security doors to the secretary who ushered me to the office pastor in charge of the outreach department. She offered me coffee, if I remember correctly. I declined, but had the presence of mind to not look around for a heavy box. The office décor was like something out of a Gothic vampire novel—dark walls, gargoyle bookends, ancient-looking maps, and a broadsword resting ominously on the counter behind an immaculate desk. Yes, a broadsword.

The pastor was very friendly, but busy. He started firing questions about my experience with STM. I had no idea why he was interested in my opinion, but I did have some thoughts about STM. Instead of boring him with stories about 4x4s and ill-timed naps, I decided to tell him what he could do to improve his STM program at the church. This, in retrospect, was exactly the right thing to say at the right time to the right person. It's not that I was shrewd; I was genuinely clueless that this was a job interview.

Apparently the youth pastor had given my name to the outreach pastor as a candidate to take over the STM department. The incumbent intern was moving on, and his replacement needed to be someone who could balance a budget. One thing you have to know about missions is when you are dealing with other people's donated money, you need a cheap, stingy miser in charge of spending. Being a destitute seminoid was valuable training in how to pinch all the spending power out of a penny. I failed accounting in high school. Literally. But I had grown to understand the basic principle that you can't spend more than you make, and I had a deep appreciation for the preciousness of donated funds. My seminary education had been subsidized by many gracious sponsors, some of whom were not wealthy, just generous.

I precociously suggested to the outreach pastor several ideas that had been floating around in my psyche like soggy driftwood. I have subsequently cleaned them up and built five maxims of STM trips with long-term impact.

1. Start with the Bible to build a philosophy of STM.
2. Select the right target (build the trip around the missionary's needs).
3. Select the right location.

4. Select the right team.
5. Train the STMers thoroughly.

So the interview was going swimmingly, until he told me it was an interview. I suddenly got nervous and sensed my audacity at suggesting improvements to the department. I felt very underdressed, underqualified, and overly critical about the department I was supposed to be passionate about. The most awkward question I faced was, "What are your weaknesses?" Everyone knows that you are supposed to say something like, "My weakness is that I work too hard, I am hard on myself when I don't perform, and I tend to sacrifice my social life for my work," or something else that makes the boss think you really want the job. But I decided to be honest. My real weakness was an uncanny absence of all administrative skills. (I had conquered my napping problem by this stage; turns out it wasn't just laziness, I also had blood-sugar problems, which I had learned to regulate through diet.) He asked me if I realized that the job was almost entirely administration. I tried to patch up the damage with assertions about being a fast learner or something. Anyway, I thought the interview was a waste of his time, but perhaps something about my ideas for how to improve the STM program would make sense to him and he would tell the guy they hired to implement some of it.

A few days later I got the callback with questions about if the offered pay was acceptable to me. Since it was double what I was making in the library, included tuition, a trip overseas, and coffee, and since I was about to be married, they could have added cleaning the sewers to my job description and I would have accepted.

I suddenly found myself with a fund that was over $20,000 in the red; 120 people to select, train, and send overseas to missionaries all over the world; and absolutely no idea what I was doing. So I turned to the best manual on missions ever written: the New Testament.

2

EST. AD 33: THE BRILLIANCE OF THE BIBLICAL PATTERN

The modern STM movement is not an untimely born brainchild of creative Christian innovators. God's own design for the church includes interdependence among churches that require travel, networking, and mutual support. Since Jesus' Great Commission for Christians to go into all nations, making disciples, baptizing, and teaching, a church's desire to plant, support, and equip other distant churches is part of the DNA of the body of Christ. The compelling instinct to spread the gospel message and plant it firmly in foreign lands runs in our ecclesiastical blood. And the STM trip is as vital to the sustenance of the universal church as the circulatory system is to the human body. It is the STM team that transports resources, doctrine, encouragement, and assistance to the outlying members of the worldwide church body.

Since STM trips are God's idea, not man's, it follows that we should consult God's Word for the methods as well as the mandate for global missions. The Bible contains a wealth of timeless wisdom to help us formulate a strategy for obtaining long-term results from STM trips. God's wisdom always transcends the trendy and pragmatic methods that our finite human think tanks can spawn. As we observe the methods and priorities of the early church, we find that a blueprint for STM philosophy emerges.

BIG BANG: THE BIRTH OF THE UNIVERSAL CHURCH

The church was born with a bang on Pentecost. The very first church was located in Jerusalem and consisted of the raw material of eleven apostles and a dense mass of visiting Jews from all over the known world. These Jews had made the annual pilgrimage to Jerusalem for the feast of the Passover, and had either lingered or returned fifty days later for the feast of Pentecost. When the Holy Spirit manifested tongues of fire and the gift of foreign languages, the crowd congregated around the spectacle of the Galilean polyglots.

Peter's Pentecost preaching challenged these Jews to confess that they had crucified their Messiah. This sermon was the catalyst to their breathtaking response of repentance and commitment to Christ, as recorded in Acts 2. The number of committed followers of Jesus exploded from 120 to three thousand, and shortly to five thousand.

This new church displayed the beautiful, untouched simplicity of the gospel in action, through caring for widows; selecting deacons; and remaining devoted to teaching, prayers, and the breaking of bread. It was a utopian scene in many respects, but one thing was, understandably, lacking. The church had no missions department.

The Jewish nation had traditionally attracted converts, not pursued them. With the exception of Jonah's extraordinary experience, Jewish history had been almost entirely about maintaining a God-ordained holy huddle to be a magnet for curious Gentiles. Jews were not a missionary people. The church, however, was left with explicit marching orders from her Lord as he departed.

Go therefore and make disciples of all nations, baptizing them in the name of the Father and of the Son and of the Holy Spirit, teaching them to observe all that I have commanded you. And behold, I am with you always, to the end of the age. (Matt 28:19,20)

The church had no precedent for this, no organizational structure, and no strategy of how to turn the world upside down with its new message. But it did not take long for the innate mobility of the gospel message to overcome the inertia of inexperience. God's providence unceremoniously nudged the fledgling church out of its cozy nest of comfort with a sudden gust of persecution.

The launch of Christian missions was fueled by and lubricated with the blood of the church's first martyr. The stoning of Stephen catapulted the Jerusalem church into action as persecution flung believers out of Jerusalem and scattered them throughout Europe and Asia. Wherever these fugitive saints ended up, the gospel reverberated with them. Suddenly the comfort of a blossoming megachurch in Jerusalem was transformed into countless pockets of faithful saints, coagulated in small congregations dotting the map.

With no denominational support or administrative infrastructure, these young churches found themselves malnourished from lack of doctrinal meat. Some churches had the luxury of apostles present in their congregations, and a growing stock of New Testament epistles. Other churches were comprised of a startled bevy of new believers, and not much else. Hence the need for the "haves" to share their blessings with the "have-nots" surfaced as a priority. Soon short-term excursions from the slightly more established churches to the embryonic, emerging churches began in earnest.

The verbs that the New Testament employs to describe the work of the post-Stephen church ministry are all terms describing outreach activity. We see the apostles preaching, teaching, writing, and otherwise proclaiming the message. But we also find them walking, riding, and sailing, with the gospel in tow. The church network was abuzz with the sending and receiving of messengers carrying greetings, encouragement, apostolic epistles, and doctrinal clarification.

The very existence of New Testament epistles nestled in our Bibles is evidence that those who had knowledge and resources instinctively knew they had a responsibility to reach out and share the wealth. Without the need for much prompting, the church at Antioch spontaneously sent Barnabas and Paul on a circuitous STM trip. With them they took teaching, encouragement, and sometimes funds.

Soon Paul was writing to churches in backwater towns and metropolises alike, commercial hotspots and incidental islets. His inspired parchments made the rounds to Rome, Crete, Philippi, Colossae, Ephesus, and the surrounds. He addressed friends and strangers, individuals and churches, pastors and elders. These letters were not emailed; they were physically borne in the hands of faithful messengers tasked with delivering the teaching material, the encouraging words of greeting, and on occasion the collected funds. The STM trip is a thoroughly biblical concept, and it behooves us to draw our philosophy of STM trips from Scripture. The densest compendium to STM is the chronicle of Paul's journeys in the book of Acts.

The book of Acts reads like a dramatized STM report. All that's missing is a slide show.

ONE SMALL STEP FOR MAN

If you know much about the contempt Jews harbored for Samaritans, then you would grasp the gravity of the first STM trip. We read, "Now when the apostles at Jerusalem heard that Samaria had received the word of God, they sent to them Peter and John, who came down and prayed for them that they might receive the Holy Spirit" (Acts 8:14,15 NASB).

This STM trip was not a great geographic distance, but the cultural divide was as dramatic as landing a man on the moon. For these Jewish-born Christians to hear the news of God saving Samaritans, and then promptly send a team of apostles to minister to them, shows that the Holy Spirit was working. Peter and John were instantaneously dispatched to ensure that this despised people group had the proper recognition and fellowship that an apostolic delegation accorded to them. No one could deny their authenticity once Peter and John had prayed for them to receive the Spirit and returned to deliver their report that the gift of tongues was indeed granted to them.

In South Africa, division between people groups is a way of life. The divide is not purely racial, as many assume. Whites are divided between those of Dutch descent and those of British descent. Blacks are divided by a myriad of other tribal lines. We boast nine official languages. We have two national anthems, which must be sung in four languages. We are a people fragmented by language and culture, politics and history. But geographically we all live in the same melting pot.

Our church, comprised of half a dozen racial groups, offers services in two languages, and in a nearby rural community we planted another church, which has services in Zulu. They met under a canvas canopy for years, until our congregation could afford to help them build a church building of their own. On Saturdays the white and black people from our English and Afrikaans church go and work on the construction site alongside the Zulu believers. The trip is by no means transcontinental. It takes all of ten to twelve minutes by car, depending on if the four traffic lights are favorable or not. But the cultural divide we leap over is a chasm rent by history and politics. The bemused community has been known to gossip about the construction site, where white and black, Afrikaans, English, Xhosa, and Zulu all sweat together for the church work. Peter and John's example is encouraging. A short trip can go a long way.

SAVE OUR SOUL(S)

Unabashed frugality leads some donors who support evangelistic missions to ask, "How many people could be reached?" What they mean to say is less palatable, "Is it really worth traveling all that way for small numbers of converts?" Shame on those who would voice such a crass sentiment, but answering them clearly may be a challenge. Again, Luke's record in Acts gives us the biblical perspective.

"Now an angel of the Lord said to Philip, 'Rise and go toward the south to the road that goes down from Jerusalem to Gaza.' This is a desert place. And he rose and went. And there was an Ethiopian" (Acts 8:26,27). The Holy Spirit led Philip to take a desert journey, to explain the gospel from the Scriptures to one man. I envy Philip's efficient travel arrangement to his next destination, Azotus, described in the following verses. Miraculous translocation seems like a better deal for STMers than the cruel and unusual legroom we are usually subjected to. If Star Trek's "beam me up" science fiction becomes science in the future, I'm sure exegetes will use that verse to justify using the technology to avoid airline food.

MEDICAL MISSIONS

Bear in mind that Luke was a physician. I'm sure it warmed his heart that some of the STM trips he wrote about were essentially medical missions trips. Today we send qualified nurses and doctors to regions where medical attention is sparse. This stewardship of their time, training, and money is a valuable offering to those whose spiritual needs can be met through the channel of meeting their physical needs. In Acts 9:32–43 Peter is traveling and heals a paralytic and raises Tabitha from the dead.

The point of Peter's ministry was to make a way for the gospel. Medical trips are not missions if they don't carry an equal dose of soul-saving gospel alongside their lifesaving antibiotics.

UNREACHED PEOPLE

Another valid target group we will examine in later chapters are unreached people groups. There are presently approximately 2 billion people who belong to people groups that have not heard the gospel. In Acts 10 Peter evangelizes an unreached people group: Gentiles.

And when the acceptance of Gentiles was related to the Jews, they were nonplussed, but quickly came around and praised God. What followed were immediate missionary journeys to investigate and initiate missions to the unreached people.

> When they heard these things they fell silent. And they glorified God, saying, "Then to the Gentiles also God has granted repentance that leads to life.
> Now those who were scattered because of the persecution that arose over Stephen traveled as far as Phoenicia and Cyprus and Antioch, speaking the word to no one except Jews. But there were some of them, men of Cyprus and Cyrene, who on coming to Antioch spoke to the Hellenists also, preaching the Lord Jesus. And the

hand of the Lord was with them, and a great number who believed turned to the Lord. The report of this came to the ears of the church in Jerusalem, and they sent Barnabas to Antioch. (Acts 11:18–22)

The Apostle Paul was expressly commissioned to be the apostle to the Gentiles (Rom 11:13). Acts 15:22,23 tells of this historic ordination to foreign missions:

Then it seemed good to the apostles and the elders, with the whole church, to choose men from among them and send them to Antioch with Paul and Barnabas. They sent Judas called Barsabbas, and Silas, leading men among the brothers, with the following letter: "The brothers, both the apostles and the elders, to the brothers who are of the Gentiles in Antioch and Syria and Cilicia, greetings."

Someone once asked Charles Spurgeon, "Will the heathen who have never heard the Gospel be saved?" Spurgeon's reply turned the tables: "It is more a question with me whether we who have the Gospel and fail to give it to those who have not can be saved."

LOCAL BELIEVERS

Sometimes our team will get there and will not get to preach the gospel to anyone. No unreached people live there, and no unbelievers arrived at the outreach event. Was the trip a failure? Was it poor stewardship, as with the lazy slave who buried his master's talent? Hardly. Another target we will examine are the local believers. It may be a valid investment of our talents to reach out to the believers of the hosting church.

As a South African new believer, my favorite time of the church calendar was when the American teams would come visit to minister and fellowship with us. It was like having a nonstop youth group meeting for three weeks.

"The report of this came to the ears of the church in Jerusalem, and they sent Barnabas to Antioch. When he came and saw the grace of God, he was glad, and he exhorted them all to remain faithful to the Lord with steadfast purpose" (Acts 11:22,23).

RETURN TO SENDER

Submission to a sending authority is a key factor in the success of any missionary endeavor, whether long term or short term. A pithy quip I once heard sagely warned, "Before a person can be a missionary, they need to be a *sub*missionary." A disgruntled lone ranger, who resigns from his church to go on a self-appointed ministry journey, is as unpredictable as a solitary elephant bull, ostracized from the herd. With no accountability or support, this untethered entity bounces around like a free radical in the body. This is not the biblical pattern.

In Acts 13:1–4 Barnabas and Saul were commissioned and sent on a journey by their home church. Your Bible might have as a subheading, "Paul's First Missionary Journey," but it should be "Paul's First STM Trip." The two delegates preach and evangelize, gather information and bring encouragement, and then in Acts 15:4, significantly, they return to their sending authority and report back to the elders what God was doing.

The STM report is not a Sunday service filler. It is a biblical requirement.

REPEAT THE SOUNDING JOY

As brief as a visit is, periodic return trips reinforce personal relationships and ministry ties that can last a lifetime. The mere presence of those who come back speaks volumes. In Acts 15:36 we see this modeled, "And after some days Paul said to Barnabas, 'Let us return and visit the brothers in every city where we proclaimed the word of the Lord, and see how they are.'"

QUALITY TIME

By far the most cynical objection to short-term trips is the question, "Can any substantial ministry really be accomplished in three weeks?" Obviously it would be fruitless to parachute into a random jungle, yell the gospel message in English for three weeks, and then get sky lifted out again. But in a strategic setting where there is a lifetime missionary who knows the language and the people, and pastors a good solid church, the short-term trip is merely a bulwark of support for the greater work.

This is evident in Acts 17:1–4:

> Now when they had passed through Amphipolis and Apollonia, they came to Thessalonica, where there was a synagogue of the Jews. And Paul went in, as was his custom, and on three Sabbath days he reasoned with them from the Scriptures, explaining and proving that it was necessary for the Christ to suffer and to rise from the dead, and saying, "This Jesus, whom I proclaim to you, is the Christ." And some of them were persuaded and joined Paul and Silas, as did a great many of the devout Greeks and not a few of the leading women.

Paul's mission field was primarily (at first) cities with established synagogues, where theologically astute Jews were gathering to worship. The STM trips lasted as little as three weeks, but accomplished much because of the foundation that was already laid. Later, when the apostle ventured to establish churches in the unreached Gentile areas, he opted for longer trips, and then functioned as a host to STM teams that came to him.

SUPPORT LETTERS ARE BIBLICAL

Thanks to STM trips, most churchgoers are accustomed to receiving the perennial support letter. The euphemistic term for this solicitation is a "prayer letter," and usually includes—alongside the check-box option of "I commit to support the team with a donation of $_____"—the obligatory option of "I commit to pray." But this is a cynical sentiment. Prayer is a key part of the success of any service to God. The trip is attempting to wage spiritual warfare, advance the gospel, serve the saints, and bring the shining light of the gospel into this present darkness. Is it not appropriate to harness the prayer support of spiritual partners in the faith?

Paul didn't hesitate to publicize his need for prayer, in Romans 15:30 he asked unabashedly, "I appeal to you, brothers, by our Lord Jesus Christ and by the love of the Spirit, to strive together with me in your prayers to God on my behalf."

Prayer is an integral part of supporting an STM trip, but so is cash. In heaven we won't need money (or STM trips, for that matter), but until then, transport, accommodations, teaching material, and other resources cost money. It is unfair to expect members of the STM team to provide for their own expenses while they are serving in the ministry the church has sent them to do (1 Cor 9). It is also not practical; it would lead to only the wealthiest church members being able to serve in this way. Surely it is easy to see that the most gifted, called, and equipped members should be considered for a spot on the team despite their lackluster savings account.

Some folks feel guilty asking for financial support from relatives and friends in the church, especially if they can afford to finance the trip themselves. But asking for help is a way of exhibiting humility and interdependence. Partnership also provides an opportunity for those who wish to participate in the team's ministry to do so in a tangible way.

It is helpful to recognize that the precedent for STM support letters is biblical. We take our cue from Paul. In Romans 15:24 Paul says frankly, "I hope to see you in passing as I go to Spain, and to be helped on my journey there by you, once I have enjoyed your company for a while." The phrase "helped on my journey there by you" is a thinly veiled request for financial support of the apostolic STM trip to Spain. Granted, our letters are a little more to the point than Paul's epistle to the Romans, but we ask for prayer and support in the same dependence on God and his saints.

GOSPEL TO GO

It is important to remember that a church's STM trip is not a Christian version of humanitarian aid. The Peace Corps, Red Cross, and countless other organizations can and do send volunteers to meet the dire physical needs of desperate people. The work of the STM team may overlap in many cases. We are to be salt and light to a watching world, and meet the physical needs of our neighbors. But what makes the STM trip unique is that it consists of Christians who are carrying the life-giving gospel to the world. This is the main goal of the church on earth, and since the STM is an extension of the local church's ministry, supporting evangelism is the main goal of the STM trip. This is not to say that every STM trip will engage in active evangelism, but they will all be a part of a greater strategy—usually one designed by the missionary and his sending authorities—which has as its aim to reach the lost with the gospel.

The primary cargo of the ambulant ministers in the book of Acts was the "word of truth, the gospel" as Paul calls the life-giving message in Colossians 1:5. The gospel is an explosive force of change in lives, hope in despair, and joy in trials. The apostles knew this. They didn't spend much time on innovating methodology. They treated the truth like a potent hand grenade. Their ministry was one of pulling the pin and flinging the gospel as far as their reach allowed. Everything in missions must undergird the goal of propagating the gospel. This pattern should inform the path our STM planning takes. The spread of the gospel is what brings lasting change to individuals and societies. STM trips must serve this cause, but supporting the work that is being done by missionaries the world over.

The more closely we pattern missions after our pioneering apostolic forefathers, the less likely we are to get bogged down in methodology, and can rather focus on the essence of the task: supporting the spread of the gospel.

3

READY, AIM, FIRE,
AND PREFERABLY IN THAT ORDER:
THE PURPOSE OF STM

In 1492 Columbus sailed the ocean blue. That little ditty has helped many historically challenged kindergarteners cement the date of the discovery of America into popular consciousness. But a comprehensive and true-to-life rhyme of Christopher Columbus' success would read more like a dissonant tale by the Brothers Grimm. The iconic explorer commanded almost no skills besides sailing a ship. He could travel far, but rarely to where he was aiming, and upon arrival was never quite sure how to make the most of the accomplishment. A well-known popular historian commented wryly,

"It would be hard to name any figure in history who has achieved more lasting fame with less competence."[5]

Resolutely aiming his fleet at the Orient, Columbus inadvertently stumbled upon South America, believing it to be India, which explains why natives in the Americas were dubbed "Indians." He then haphazardly explored this area for about eight years, bumping into various Caribbean Islands, which he pertinaciously continued to label as Oriental. He mistook the island of Cuba for mainland Asia, and he neglected to actually set foot in America, the territory most people assume he discovered. Throughout his voyage he gleefully loaded his flotilla with copious amounts of fool's gold and prodigious quantities of random plant matter that were in his estimation highly valuable spices from the East. Upon his return to Europe, as part of their exotic cargo, his surviving crew delivered their own dubious contribution to the Old World—namely, syphilis.

Nevertheless, Christopher Columbus undeniably changed the world forever. By establishing contact with the New World and lugging unknown foodstuffs back home, he began an irreversible historical movement of seismic proportions, the social, political, economic aftershocks of which are still being felt today. The quake would significantly affect church history.

The colonization of the Americas brought all the violence, exploitation, and disease that accompanies conquest and invasion, but it also established a bridge for the gospel. In a real sense, Christopher Columbus unwittingly started a chain of events that would lead to a geographic explosion of the gospel.

Unfathomable consequences and astonishing good can come from misdirected voyages.

In a similar way an STM trip can be microcosm of the Columbian Exchange. A poorly aimed trip has the potential to wreak cultural and spiritual havoc in a village in Africa, or it can create a lasting bridge for the gospel to bring hope and change that echoes in eternity.

No one is discounting the testimonies of tremendous good that has been done by STM teams with no clue as to what they were meant to be accomplishing. God uses bent and blunt instruments because there is no other kind available among mankind. But the saving grace of a bumbling human

---

5   Bill Bryson, *At Home* (London: Transworld, 2010), 254.

race is the prerogative to learn from our mistakes and adjust the course of future endeavors. Just imagine how much more benefit could come from an intentional, organized, goal-oriented STM trip.

TAKING AIM

STM trips are the arrows of kingdom warfare. The team represents the long-distance effort of local churches to reach the nations for Jesus. I have found that the excitement of an STM trip often leads to a church firing its arrows off into the distance without much concern for how they land. The first change I made to my new department was to shift the crosshairs of our efforts over to the correct target: the missionary.

STM is not missions. Missions is when a person gives up their life and immerses themselves in a foreign culture to understand it, communicate with it, and redeem it. All the present-day discussion about "missional" churches is just semantic jerry-rigging of the English language to make hip and trendy what has always been plain-vanilla Christianity. Living in your hometown and being a good witness, kind neighbor, and model citizen is not "missional," it's Christian. Missions, as our language has always defined it, is not a sedentary concept, but a mobile one. Missions is to *go* make disciples of all the nations, to take the message elsewhere. And the further you take it, the more you need to "become all things to all people" as Paul did (1 Cor 9:22), and the more you need to adapt. But STM is just a side dish to complement that meal; it isn't the whole menu.

Two weeks abroad can't possibly have the same impact as a full-time missionary can over the long haul. As obvious as this may sound, some churches do not send missionaries, they send STMers and check "missions" off on their religious to-do list. Missions is when called, highly trained, and church-commissioned Christians and their households rip themselves from the comfort, familiarity, and sometimes safety of home for one glorious purpose—to fling the gospel to another corner of God's kingdom. They plant a flag, a tree, and themselves, and say "We are here to stay." To honor a ten-day trip to dig wells in Africa with the coveted title "missions" is to smudge the value of the missionaries' sacrifices. Our job is to hold the ropes and call it that, or something other than doing missions. So what function does the STM trip perform in the grand work of global missions?

There are many benefits to an STM, but the real question is, what should the center of the target be? The other beneficiaries are the other circles, but who is the bull's eye? Have you ever heard of a "Texan target"? Picture a barn wall with a series of targets painted on it, each one with a single bullet hole in the dead center. Impressive right? Until you see how the shooter first shoots at the barn and then paints the target around the hole. This is what a lot of churches do. Whatever their STM departments currently do, they declare is the goal of the STM trip, instead of deciding from Scripture what the center should be and then aiming their arsenal of resources at the biblical bull's eye.

There are five different zones of influence that STM trips can impact. These five targets that STM trips should regard as the bull's eye are: (1) the travelers (whom we will call STMers), (2) the sending church, (3) the local unbelievers, (4) the receiving church, and (5) the missionaries who receive. Every trip will impact several if not all of these targets. The issue is, which target is primary; which one should the bull's eye be?

THE STMERS

Some STM departments are unabashedly member focused. These remind me of the old US Navy recruitment posters, "Join the Navy, see the world," as if the entire US armada exists for the primary purpose of getting its young men some stamps in their passports.

The sending church will in this case invariably highlight the personal benefits one can expect from joining. This is easy to do because an STM trip certainly does impact those serving on the team. It is no exaggeration to say your life will be changed if you serve in an STM team. Your spiritual life will undoubtedly get an adrenaline boost of enthusiasm. You will definitely have a more global mindset, you will understand better how God works in different cultures, you may forge lifelong friendships with other team members and the foreigners you serve. And yes, you may even meet your future spouse on the trip. And there is nothing sinful in that. It is more blessed to give than receive, so we should expect that our service would leave us royally blessed beyond our expectations. But are these benefits the *reason* for the trip, or are they simply part of the *reward*?

The STM trip is not a spiritual sightseeing trip; it is not Christianized tourism. NASA doesn't exist because Neil Armstrong wanted to start a moon-rock collection. Armstrong's experience was an undeniable privilege, but I'm sure we can all agree that there were bigger goals at play than his personal travel aspiration. The STM trip will provide lasting personal enrichment, but those factors should be kept in proper perspective. Your wanderlust is not a good enough reason to apply for an STM trip.

The fallout of this motive driving an applicant is that his or her expectations are primarily focused on anticipated experience. So when things fall apart, as they tend to do with alarming regularity in international travel, the STMer feels disappointed. Likewise, those who are craving a hard-core adventure of altruistic service for the suffering natives of Africa are sometimes shocked by how well off these supposedly shivering hordes really are. Mud huts with satellite dishes and flat screen TV's are not uncommon in rural Africa.

An STM team from the UK came to minister alongside our church in South Africa. One STMer was honest enough to confess his surprise at the lack of misery he encountered among our congregation. Most of our flock lived in nicer houses than his own, some were better educated than him, and several more widely traveled. Even when he ventured into the more rural community, he was stunned to find that the poor unfortunates he came to comfort all had mounted on their drafty, corrugated shanty houses satellite dishes —a luxury his own family coveted. Whether the reality of the trip turns out to be much better or way worse than anticipated, the STMer now feels cheated out of their experience. If their report back reflects this disillusionment, they can adversely affect future teams' fund-raising. A congregation that feels their contribution was a waste of money will be less likely to support a future trip. And this all because the traveler was wrongly told the trip would benefit him or her in a particular way.

THE SENDING CHURCH

When a church is blessed with some enthusiastic saint who has a vision to lead the very first STM trip in the church's history, the initial obstacle is the treasurer, or whichever committee feels sovereign over balancing the church's accounts. This is a tough first assignment for Joe Visionary. Ecclesiastical wheels grind slowly, and the lubricating oil is cash. There is no way to sell the idea of STM from a financial angle. This trip is never going to bring in money. It is going to pick the very pockets needed to make the church budget. Unlike other ministries in the church, this one won't bring in new members in the long run; its evangelism will benefit some other faraway church and their treasurer. It doesn't increase the church's community profile. So what's in it for us? It is sad, but it's what most STMers are up against.

So the selling points of the trip are often phrased in the form of intangible profits to the sending church. For example, the promise that the usual pew-warming youth will be roped into actual ministry, and there will be slide shows to prove it. Or the prediction that the church will get a renewed sense of global missions and perhaps even feel like they are contributing to the Great Commission. Upon their return the STMers will be on fire for ministry and we can plug them into teaching Sunday school or visiting widows with their slide shows. In fact, we can make it mandatory for team members to attend whatever classes the elders teach, thus boosting numbers at the waning Wednesday night lectures.

Again, it is true that a church that sends STMers abroad will be the recipient of many blessings. It is better to give than receive. No really. But again, do we want to foster that mindset in our church?

The stark truth is that "doing church" is not primarily about doing ministry. The mission of the church is not about merely meeting a budget successfully, it's not about keeping people happy or fulfilled, and it's not even firstly about local evangelism.

Church is about the glory of God. Church is about Jesus. The STM trip will bring glory to God by serving missionaries who are occupied with the kingdom work of reaching the nations. And that should be all the sales pitch any ministry needs. These types of churches need to get over themselves and realize that STMs are profitable for the kingdom of God. And conversely the STM trip should not be focused primarily on the benefits it will bring to the sending church.

THE LOCAL UNBELIEVERS

Every evangelical Christian by definition is one who wants to share the gospel with the lost. Charles Spurgeon articulated well the passion that resides in the bosom of every mature saint:

> If sinners be damned, at least let them leap to Hell over our dead bodies. And if they perish, let them perish with our arms wrapped about their knees, imploring them to stay. If Hell must be filled, let it be filled in the teeth of our exertions, and let not one go unwarned and unprayed for.[6]

This compulsion to reach the lost causes some to miss the true objective of short-term trips. Sometimes what makes a location an attractive option for an STM team is the dearth of a gospel presence. The team will target a region in which there is no church, thinking that they are preaching in an area where Christ is not being proclaimed. Though this target is certainly more noble than those mentioned above, it is naïve to believe the most significant impact of an STM trip can be made on this type of field. What has happened in this scenario is that a location that is ripe for a long-term missionary has been wrongly chosen for only a short-term effort.

Evangelism does not work best in an environment where there is no prior context of teaching, no relationship to the audience, and no follow-up system. Yes, Peter preached Christ to strangers at Pentecost, but these were Jews who had a context in which to fit the preaching of the Messiah they heard from Peter, who was also a Jew. They shared a common respect for the Old Testament Scriptures as a source of authority. This is not the case, necessarily, when an STM team arrives in a location with no church.

Many polytheists would gladly accept Jesus as another one of their many lords and saviors. The team might not even know that their preaching has done more harm than good by creating false assurance and expanding a syncretistic religion.

---

6 Charles Spurgeon, "The Wailing of Risca," a sermon delivered at Exeter Hall, London, December 9, 1860. Print version found in *The Metropolitan Pulpit, Vol. 7,* sermon 349.

It is certainly possible that someone, even many people, may hear the gospel and repent of their sins and get saved, but then what? Christians who descend on an unchurched region, drop the gospel bomb without any context, and then are promptly beamed back up to their mother ship are fooling themselves if they think they are fulfilling the Great Commission.

Jesus said to go, baptize, *and teach* them!

The most you are doing in a hit-and-run STM evangelism trip, if anyone is genuinely saved, is to create a community of spiritual orphans. You make baby Christians and leave them to fend for themselves. You have just provided ready prey for the serpent or, like the Jungle Book toddler, to be raised by wolves and therefore behave like them in later life.

The best way to reach an unbeliever is to plug them into a local church. Since an STM cannot possibly be expected to plant a church, with a biblical leadership, and a body of doctrine intact within three weeks or so, the local unbelievers are not a viable target group at which to aim an STM trip. If a team really does want to impact unbelievers with the gospel, it needs to do so in the context of a local church, which leads to the next potential target, the receiving church.

THE RECEIVING CHURCH

Now we are getting closer to the bull's eye. Paul's missionary journeys were often meant to strengthen churches. The ministry of the STM should be more for the benefit of others than for that of the STMers or sending church. This comes with some basic implications that are frequently overlooked. First, the trip should be more of a help than a burden to the receiving church. If that sounds obvious to you, I challenge you to ask churches that have received teams if this is always the case. Sometimes churches decide to send teams to their missionaries, and the missionaries feel obligated to accommodate them, sometimes at considerable expense in finances and manpower.

But the receiving church can also be hugely blessed if the team is assembled well. If most of the team members are spiritually mature, selfless servants, the local believers will be encouraged by their example, and the church will benefit from the joy of hosting like-minded strangers. Hebrews 13:2 commands Christians to be hospitable to strangers, and Hebrews 10:24

commands all believers to encourage one another. The STM is the single stone that whacks both birds.

The danger is when the team is not focused enough on being helpful and is too enamored with what they are going to get out of the experience. Also, if team leaders get desperate for numbers, the standard is lowered and spiritual tadpoles end up leading adult Bible studies in a foreign culture, when they would not yet be allowed to teach kids in their home church.

The receiving church is a worthy target for the STM arrow, but there is one better.

The core philosophy of STM, which this book strives to explain, is that the whole STM world revolves around the axis of the missionary, his family, his ministry, and his strategy. The understanding of the missionary's role is so pivotal that it warrants its own chapter.

4

STRANGER IN A STRANGE LAND: THE MISSIONARY IS THE MISSION

I had never been called an alien before I came to America to attend The Master's Seminary. I was born, raised, and educated in the Republic of South Africa. With my citizenship came certain rights and privileges in my homeland, none of which brought me much comfort at JFK airport. As I disembarked after the longest commercial flight on the planet, from Johannesburg to New York City, I was immediately struck by an interesting image. After an uninterrupted twenty-four hours of enduring cruel and unusual legroom, hundreds of fatigued passengers were waddling through customs and immigrations in two distinct lines. One line was an overcrowded mass; it was congested and slow moving, like gridlock traffic. The other line was a jet stream of efficiency. It zipped through customs with the pace of a carpool lane. Individuals with sleek briefcases and blue passports were confidently striding through the line marked "American Citizens Only." I had read about the narrow way and the broad way in Scripture, but I had never seen it enacted so literally before! As I stood in a sea of tourists toting green passports and travel guides, I glanced up at the sign above our line. It read, "Alien Citizens."

As Christians our citizenship is in heaven (Phil 3:20). We are all aliens and strangers in this world (1 Pet 2:11). None, however, experience the isolation of being foreign as our missionaries do. Not only are they aliens to this world, but they are literally strangers in a strange land. In addition to their spiritual foreignness, they experience a cultural, social, and often linguistic foreignness as well.

STM is a way of ministering to these faithful missionaries. Just as Paul sent Timothy to strengthen and encourage the Thessalonians as to their faith (1 Thess 3:2), we send out small teams of believers to bring encouragement. We bring a "slice of home" to them. We bring the good and pleasant balm of sweet fellowship. Our missionaries are refreshed and revived by spending time with believers from their home church, believers who pray for them, love them, and understand them.

It is the long-term, faithful persistence of missionaries with dogged tenacity that brings the most lasting results. As William Carey once modestly offered, "I can plod. I can persevere in any definite pursuit. To this I owe everything."[7] It is the silent plodding of endurance in the face of difficulties that shouts louder than the lip service of loquacious short-term preachers.

It takes a brave soul to leave the security of home. The novelty of going off to college is often tempered by the pangs of isolation and unfamiliarity in the first lonely month. The joy of a businessman's first overseas company trip is often accompanied by the poignant dissonance he feels about leaving his precious family for those two eternal weeks. And the adrenalin of patriotism that burns in the veins of young soldiers is always chilled by the realization that they must leave their homeland for an indefinite tour. What would drive a family to leave the warmth, the comfort, and the security of their home?

The answer is not a simple one, but there is an impulse in all Christians that moves us to take the torch of the gospel to others, even if it means

---

7   Eustace Carey, *Memoir of William Carey, D. D.* (London: Jackson & Walford, 1836), 623.

stepping outside of our comfort zones. For some, that may be peering over the cubicle in the office and striking up a friendship that will open doors for the gospel. For others, it may mean packing up all their possessions and moving permanently to remote cultures. For some it means learning their neighbors' names; for others it means learning their language.

Not everyone has the gift and calling to permanently relocate to a foreign field, but there is still an integral way they can be involved in bringing and proclaiming the gospel to others . . . enter Short-term Missions. STM takes the soothing balm of fellowship and encouragement to our missionaries. Our missionaries are our mission!

A UNIQUE BREED

The Mont-Joux pass is the erstwhile name of a particularly treacherous mountain pass in the Alps between Switzerland and Italy. For centuries thousands of people lost their lives trying to cross it in winter. When a snowstorm unpredictably arose, there would be a whiteout, and with no way to stay on course travelers would get lost and freeze to death.

But, suddenly, in the 1700s the death rate declined drastically. The reason was not due to any technological advances. The climate hadn't changed. The reason the death rate declined was due to a dog, or to be more accurate, a breed of dogs. This canine had an uncanny aptitude for navigation in the blinding fog, an incredible stamina in below-freezing temperatures, and an almost mystical ability to locate freezing people in the snow.

By this stage the pass was named for the monastery founded by Saint Bernard of Mont-Joux, so naturally the dogs were also canonized as Saint Bernards.

During the two hundred or so years that the faithful "saints" served on the Saint Bernard Pass, over two thousand lost souls were rescued from the frostbitten clutches of an icy death. The way they would rescue the frozen traveler was this: first, they would find them in the snow, delivering a lifesaving supply of whiskey and bread in barrels, which they carried around their necks; and second, they would lead the way back to the monastery.

The rescue dog breed is an apt metaphor for missionaries. These are a breed of believer that exhibits extraordinary stamina and perseverance, exceptional abilities to find needs to meet, but they are also powerless to help the lost soul, except for delivering the life-giving elixir, in this case the gospel message.

These are men and women who are never content with the *status quo* that creeps over the church. They sense the urgency in Christ's Great Commission to reach the world.

Missionary C. T. Studd captured this sentiment in his clever couplet: "Some wish to live within the sound of a chapel bell; I wish to run a rescue mission within a yard of hell."

William Carey also articulated this with his probing, eighty-seven page "An Enquiry into the Obligation of Christians to use Means for the Conversion of the Heathen" published in 1792. His "Enquiry" was an interrogation directed at those who had grown comfortable in their introspective religiosity, exploring whether the Great Commission of the Lord was still binding on his generation. He felt the urge to extend God's kingdom in ways that left many of his contemporaries nonplussed. He exulted in the closing of the "Enquiry," with this enraptured motivation: "What a treasure, what a harvest must await such characters as Paul and John Eliot and David Brainerd, and others, who have given themselves wholly to God's work! What a heaven will it be to see the myriads of the heathen, of Britons among the rest, who by their labours have been brought into the knowledge of God! Surely such a crown of rejoicing deserves our aspiration! Surely it is worthwhile to lay ourselves out with all out might in promoting Christ's kingdom!"[8]

All who receive the call of God to full-time missions on their lives empathize with that compulsion, including the Apostle Paul, who explained his personal preference as an itinerant missionary: "And thus I make it my ambition to preach the gospel, not where Christ has already been named, lest I build on someone else's foundation" (Rom 15:20).

A UNIQUE NEED

Carey volunteered for his pioneering mission to India with this challenge to his supporters: "I am willing to go into the pit, if you will hold the ropes."

---

8   S. Pearce Carey, *William Carey,* 71.

He did not merely mean finances. A strong rope is made of many strands. Money is only one aspect of support the missionary needs in order to fulfill his ministry.

My position at Grace Community allowed me the immense privilege of rubbing shoulders with dozens of missionaries as they came home on furlough, or as I met them abroad in their homes. I learned that they need what every Christian needs, only more of it, because they spend most of their lives pouring out energy to meet the needs of others. Missionaries need prayer, fellowship, encouragement, babysitters, books, edifying conversations, theological stimulation, advice, an audience for their stories, a shoulder to drench. Missionaries need what you need. A monthly check is a paltry excuse for a rope.

The STM is one of the best ways of meeting the missionary's needs. The team is a care package of human resources we send our frontline troops. These people live in the bull's eye of the STM target. These are the folks who have given up their family, friends, the comforts of home, the ease of the mother tongue, the convenience of citizenship, and many other sacrifices you and I will never understand. They know their field better than you ever can. They are savvy as to how things work and what to avoid. They are *au fait* with the culture and have insight into what will help or hinder the mission of spreading the gospel. It is beyond arrogant, it is absurd to expect that an STM team, with their training measured not in years but in hours, could make the lasting impact that missionaries strive for. The best the STM team can hope for is to help the missionaries in their goals, and try not to mess things up too much.

If this sounds like I have a low view of STMs, let me clarify. I take a dim view of teams that assume they are God's gift to the mission field. I have a high regard for a team that understands that the missionary is the boss. Some sincere but ignorant believers completely misunderstand the needs of their missionaries.

NEITHER HERE NOR THERE

Missionaries are expected to be cultural chameleons. Remaining too foreign may be detrimental to their acceptance in a new community. But if they acculturate too wholesale, they are open to ignorant family members back home accusing them of "forgetting their roots" or being unpatriotic. How wise can it be for an American missionary ministering in an Arab country to fly the Stars and Stripes in his front yard? How effective can a Western missionary serving in Japan be if he refuses to join his new church's elders in the public bathhouse for a leadership meeting?

Diplomatic emissaries are transferred to a new field every four years. But missionaries often spend decades at a time in a particular location. Unlike political diplomats, their job is to integrate enough into the culture to be able to effect change in the lives of locals, by sharing with them the culturally transcendent truth of the gospel. And yet their support will come from their home country, from people who will expect them to pop in and say "hi" when they are on furlough. In order to relate to the supporters, the missionary has to switch gears back into the culture of the sending church. They have to have conversations with people who hold the financial purse strings, but who sometimes have no idea what it is like to live as a foreigner.

Missionaries are perpetually strangers in a strange land.

But the most conflicted of the missionary subgroups are the MKs (what we affectionately call "missionary kids"). Missionary's children are sometimes termed "third culture kids" since they do not fit in perfectly in the culture of their parent's chosen field, but neither are they at home in the culture of their citizenship. They have missed the pop-culture references their peer group imbibes daily from the local media. They are new to trends that are already outdated. One MK confided in me that he only feels at home in airports and on planes. Although he has lived in his parent's ministry field for his entire life, and speaks the native language fluently, he is still viewed as a foreigner by his peers. When he returns home for brief furlough stints, he is out of touch with the trends and slang of his age group. The TV shows and the sports stats that his own culture is *au fait* with are virtually unknown to him. Only in airports is he not keenly aware of not blending in, since everyone else is at that moment also neither here nor there.

I had the privilege of serving on an STM team in Spain. The task we were given was to host a VBS, not for Spanish children, but for the children of the American missionaries who were attending a conference in Barcelona. The missionaries were serving in various fields in Europe, and some of them barely knew each other. The mix of children we encountered surprised me. Though they were all American by citizenship, they were distinctly European in their dress, demeanor, and interests. This was brought home to me when I watched them playing cricket and rugby on the beach instead of baseball and football. One youngster had an impassioned debate with another, and as their emotions took over, they both flipped their language to the French channel. Apparently the French language is more conducive to spirited disagreement than their native English. But they were not European. They were American. They celebrated July 4th and Bastille Day; they supported British soccer clubs and American basketball teams.

HANDLE WITH CARE

Since the primary goal of the STM team is to hold the ropes for the missionary in the pit of a foreign field, the STM team is responsible to do what it can to understand the missionaries' needs, and then meet those needs. Missionaries look forward to a little slice of home being delivered to them in the form of an STM team. Don't disappoint them. Do not come full of the questions and expectations and insensitive comments they are bombarded with when they come home on furlough.

Do your homework by reading travel guides and getting information about the country, its population, religions, climate, cultural distinctive, and other pertinent information. You are not going to the country primarily to learn, but to serve. Remember that the goal of the trip is to help the missionary, not milk him to enhance your experience.

Perhaps the most strategic thing you can do before even assembling a team or locking down a location is to make sure your missionary has a need you can meet. The policy of an effective STM program is simple: *give the missionary what he needs.*

INTERROGATE YOUR MISSIONARY

John F. Kennedy's most memorable challenge was, "Ask not what your country can do for you, ask what you can do for your country." In a similar vein STM planners must not start by asking what is in it for the team, but begin with asking what they can do for the missionary.

Here are some questions to ask your missionary to ensure your team meets a real need:[9]

1. Do you want an STM team this year? Do not skip this question. Many churches assume that their team is God's gift to the missionary. Many missionaries, however, think of the teams as a test of their sanctification. Remember your missionary is the one who knows his field best, and some situations are volatile and require sensitivity to the culture for which untrained volunteers are not equipped.

2. When suits you? Often missionaries have a long-term strategy that would require a team at a particular time of the year suitable to their country's school calendar. Your Christmas break might not best suit a Muslim calendar, and your summer vacation period might coincide with a formidable Russian winter (quite an obstacle to outdoor street evangelism in my experience).

3. How many of us can you comfortably host? If you open your trip up to everyone who has a passport, your missionary may have to commandeer a school bus to get you home from the airport. As one who has received as well as sent STM trips I have found that it is most economical to host teams that come in increments that can legally squeeze into a minibus. That means seven or eight (with luggage) if one has an international license, ten if they are all thin. Eleven visitors bring the unwelcome expense of hiring an additional car and arranging another driver. These numbers will differ drastically from field to field, so consult your missionary before you tell applicants they are accepted.

4. What do you need us to do, and whom do you need to do it? A missionary to Ireland might not jump at your suggested group of elderly ladies qualified to teach English as a second language. He may want to run a sports outreach that year, and was hoping for your rambunctious youth group.

5. How much is this going to cost you? After gaining as much information as you can, make sure you talk about the finances. Many missionaries will not volunteer the fact that the team costs them money, unless they are pressed to

---

9   The five questions that follow are excerpted from Clint Archer, "Short-term Missions: Supporting and Directing Those We Send," in *Rediscovering Biblical Evangelism*, ed. John MacArthur (Nashville: Thomas Nelson, 2011), 301–2.

do so. Some find it unspiritual—until they have to feed an army of hungry teens. Getting an accurate estimate of what the trip will cost in-country will help you care for the missionary.

Assure your missionary that this trip will not cost him a single rupee. Horde every receipt of every tank of gas he pays for, hijack every restaurant bill before it gets to him. Come with lavish gifts for his family, and get ideas of what they need including books, baking ingredients, local magazines, and football jerseys for the kids. Please, no used tea bags.

ARRANGE AN ORIENTATION SESSION

One of the ways to avoid a constant stream of repeated dumb questions is to get them all over and done with in one session. Ask the missionary to prepare an orientation session for the team upon its arrival. This session should cover whatever the missionary considers to be important, such as any common cultural *faux pas* he wants you to avoid, theological landmines to sidestep, etc., but it should also include answering the barrage of questions your team has. This list of questions could be sent ahead of the team, so that the missionary is prepared to answer them, or he could even reply by email before the trip arrives, so as not to waste valuable time in-country.

BE A MULE

"Drug mules" are travelers who smuggle illegal narcotics across borders in some of the most creative and stomach-churning ways imaginable. Their career opportunity comes from the demand for transportation (smuggling) of goods that cannot be moved conventionally. Similarly (but not too similarly!) there are many goods that the missionary may want from his home country that are too costly to send by mail, or seem too petty for the expense they incur. Perhaps he's worn out his favorite brand of sneakers, or depleted his reserve of Starbucks coffee. A flannelgraph easel can be a commodity you take for granted until you move to the third world. The list of accoutrements we pay no mind to at home become conspicuously absent halfway around the globe. We were surprised (momentarily shocked into teary despair) when we realized that chocolate chips are unobtainable in the part of Africa to which we moved. When our yearly STM team arrives in June, it feels like Christmas for our family.

MAKE SOME NOISE

Missionaries are characteristically some of the most humble and least materialistic people in your church, and yet they are wrongly expected to spend their lives self-promoting their ministries and asking for money. This ought not to be so. Missionaries will often go decades without a real vacation, as they spend their entire furlough off the field traveling to the countless churches who each contribute a token amount to them, but require a pound of flesh in the form of a PowerPoint presentation in order to maintain the support "relationship."

The more "marketing" the STM team can do on behalf of the missionary, the better. The team can have a long-term impact on the ministry by being vocal proponents of the ministry they saw firsthand, and they can become enthusiastic fundraisers for the missionaries.

STAY IN TOUCH

Missionaries are by definition aliens. They are strangers in the land they inhabit. Some missionaries' only friends are other missionaries who happen to be in the same field. They sometimes make friends with those to whom they are ministering, but the relationship will seldom be that of peers. They get lonely. They feel isolated. When they return home, they are viewed as novelties, exotic, and asked to talk all about the country they minister in. This is exactly what happens to them in their field.

With the advent of free email services (Gmail.com), free video conferencing (e.g., Skype.com), social media websites (e.g., Facebook.com), and personal blogs, there is no excuse for leaving your missionary in a silent pit of isolation. Part of holding the ropes is to keep the communication lines taut with news, greetings, and messages of encouragement. The missionaries' prayer requests should be a regular part of your church prayer life, whether that be a section in the Sunday bulletin, or an item in the weekly prayer meeting, or any means your church employs to pray for one another. Your missionary is your family. They are part of your church. They are the part in the pit. So call out to them as you grip that rope.

5

FIELD OF DREAMS:
SELECTING A DESTINATION

Real-estate pundits know that the three most important factors in determining the value of a property are: location, location, and location.
Property speculators with foresight will purchase the most decrepit
and dilapidated building on the most overgrown and unkempt property, if
the location has promise. There's nothing a little dynamite can't fix. You can
always level the existing placeholders and rebuild the superstructure from
scratch, but you can't manufacture a breathtaking view or proximity to a
pristine beach, key freeway exit, or peaceful wildlife preserve. The problem
with this mentality, however, is that it does not apply to the spiritual world
in which missions operates.

We tend to think of geographic location as an important factor in making decisions about spiritual ministry. But much biblical wisdom must be applied when deciding where to send a team. Choosing a field of ministry is a balancing act between the general instruction God gives us to minister to the world, and the discernment required to sort through the myriad needs that present themselves all over the globe. I love what William Carey quipped concerning this balance: "To know the will of God, we need an open Bible and an open map."

A church that is situated two hours by minivan from an orphanage that needs a squad of Vacation Bible School teachers, needn't look to cross oceans simply for the sake of an exotic location. The argument could even be made that the closer the ministry is to your church, the more effective will the relationship be, as it can be kept up over time and probably has less cultural or language barriers, not to mention the expense that would be saved.

On the other hand, if a need arises in a village that is so remote that the costs and inconvenience of getting there intimidates churches who have resources, the physical location has become a spiritual stronghold to conquer.

Imagine you offered a trip to the Seychelles Islands and had to beat applicants away with a stick. Then after a team is selected you announced that the need has been met by another church, but the same need has arisen in a neighboring inner-city area. Anyone who suddenly remembers that they have bought a new plow that needs testing, and can therefore not be involved, was probably not fit for the original trip. A challenge that foreign missions faces is that some people bit by the travel bug may be attracted more to the adventure than the ministry. This leads to a world tour funded by the widow's mites.

There is nothing wrong with excitement stemming from the novelty of international travel. But the primary focus should always be the ministry. One way to assist in establishing an STM trip with its priorities right is to start with what you can offer, not what food you like (or every church would have a an annual trip destined for Italy).

An honest and thorough evaluation of what your church has to offer will guide your choice of type of ministry, which in turn will narrow down the choice of location. This order is crucial to ensuring your trip is achieving maximum impact for the kingdom. The destination should be chosen according to the current ministry presence and the type of team you could assemble in order to assist that ministry.

Here are some types of ministry with which STMs can assist local and international missionaries.

TEACHING TRIPS

If your church's forte is doctrine, you may possess a valuable commodity in the spiritual world: well-taught, doctrinally sound believers. Not everyone who knows doctrine is qualified or inclined to teach, but if you have a handful of gifted, equipped Bible teachers, the teaching team could prove to be a phenomenally effective team for long-term impact.

Churches that are located near seminaries or Bible colleges should mine the gold God has dropped on their doorstep. Seminary students need teaching experience as much as churches need teaching; it's a match made in heaven's strategic planning department. Make full use of this boon.

A missionary can stir up some attention and hoopla about an international keynote speaker headlining the family conference or youth camp his church is staging. The novelty of an imported preacher is often enough to draw substantially larger crowds than usual. This is the same mentality that drives people to eat out at a restaurant, rather than another home-cooked meal. The food isn't necessarily better; it's just different.

The pastor of the church in which I was converted was an American missionary. After a year under his preaching, the accent no longer sounded foreign to me. When I heard of an American conference speaker coming to town, I was excited to go hear him. It was only later that I realized the irony of that impulse. This was reinforced when I found out that our pastor was considered a highly sought-after conference speaker in America.

Especially effective teaching trips are those that target pastors. If you are one who thinks in terms of "bang for your buck," a pastors' conference is possibly the most efficient use of teaching resources. The exhortation, example, and equipping that a room full of pastors enjoy is multiplied many times over as the teaching trickles into the pews of all their churches. There is naturally a much higher level of theological training and practical knowledge in countries where Christianity is allowed. We have seminaries, theological bookshops, theology conferences, and many other resources with which to glut our appetite for truth. Not so in closed countries where literature and education is filtered by Big Brother governments.

My journeys to the persecuted church almost always focus on training the pastors. The leaders of churches in closed countries are not only starved of training, but they also spend their lives pouring what they do know into others, without much opportunity to reload. Encouraging these men and equipping them with doctrinal and practical training is an extremely useful way to minister to the persecuted church. A healthy flock needs a healthy shepherd.

EVANGELISM TRIPS

A newly planted church often struggles with landing in town with a splash. They are also understandably thin on manpower. Shipping them a team of vivacious evangelists may be just what the fledgling church needs to create a stir in their neighborhood. Having a visiting team of evangelists helps to boost the confidence of those in the church, and can perhaps teach and model how to do open-air, door-to-door, and other intimidating forms of evangelism. The team can be assembled to include the sending church's most seasoned evangelists. Another advantage is that it is easier for people to be bold and direct in their evangelism when they are in a foreign land for a limited time. There is a sense of urgency, and fewer inhibitions because you feel that you will never see these people again anyway. It's the same reason some singers can perform onstage in front of thousands, but are shy to sing a solo for their friends and family. This boldness sets an example and can be infectious.

On one trip my wife and I did to Northern Ireland, the local believers' confidence was enflamed when our team agreed to accompany them into a neighborhood notorious for being antagonistic to any Protestant ministry. We were literally too ignorant to be intimidated. We had no idea what was so scary about approaching this particular housing development. So we eagerly spurred the locals on, and we preached boldly over a PA system. It soon became evident why those with experience were standing behind the parked cars. The verbal abuse that was hurled at us from apartment windows was soon mingled with stones! A few whizzed by me, clanking against the car

I was next to. I got the hint and joined the savvy local believers in a spirited, wheel-spinning escape.

The great success that day was twofold. First, the gospel was proclaimed. Remember that for every rock thrower there were countless others sitting quietly at their windows listening to every word. And second, the local believers were encouraged to be bolder in their future evangelistic endeavors. All it took was a little imported naïveté to get the adrenalin for outreach pumping.

SERVICE TRIPS

This would include any ministry that simply requires manpower to help the local church accomplish its goals. Construction, Vacation Bible School, medical services, or sports ministries are prime examples, and each comes with its own challenges and opportunities. Our teams have offered services as widely ranging as soccer camps in Croatia and basketball lessons in Uganda, to vaccination clinics and dental work. These services provide a platform for potentially evangelistic relationships between the local church and the natives who attend, as well as bring attention and even perhaps credibility to the missionary's ministry. Though it is true that the services could often be arranged and funded without the team's help, there is an inherent attraction to the visiting foreigners, and the missionary's relationship with the team demonstrates tangibly to the local community that he is not a rogue self-appointed man, but has the backing of churches back home.

Service teams are focused on offering help to the missionary or community, either for practical assistance for the ministry, or as a significant gesture to the locals. There are a few different types of service teams.

Construction

Construction crews, in order to be helpful to the missionary, should meet some need that cannot be met by the local labor. Manual labor hired locally is always going to be cheaper than a team flying in from the sending church. In this case a generous cash donation would save the sending church a lot of money, and meet the need of the missionary just as well—if not better, as it is rare to find a team of churchgoers who are adequately skilled at construction.

But there are some cases where expense should be overlooked. For example, the missionary may want to be make a statement to the locals that he has support from his sending country, or he may not want to reinforce an inferiority complex the natives carry by hiring them to work for him and "call him boss" as it were. There are also some cultures in which the manual labor is considered demeaning or unnecessary.

A trip I was part of helped build a church building structure for a missionary in an African country. The local men refused to work, at any cost, because the diamond conglomerate conveniently delivered ample groceries—and more than ample alcohol—to the locals, as a strategy to keep them off their rightful lands, where the diamonds were located. The only way to build anything was to hire foreigners, so it made more sense for the sending church to supply foreigners for free in the form of our team. Construction is also often only one tiny aspect of the team's role, where the fellowship and encouragement that ensues is more valuable than the bricklaying and cement mixing that, almost incidentally, happens.

Sports Camps

Sports camps are a popular attraction for some cultures. It can be a magnet for local children to have a team of American basketball players teaching them training drills for a week, while sharing the gospel formally and informally. This ministry only works if the sport your team is offering to coach is one that the locals can relate to, while simultaneously being one with which they would appreciate the help.

Americans offering a soccer camp in Brazil may end up learning more about the game from the locals than that which they went there to teach. And offering a coaching camp of American football techniques in Malawi, where the sport is virtually unknown, would be equally redundant. As long as enough thought and planning goes into this type of trip, it can be a wonderful use of the international language of sport to bridge cultural gaps.

Medical Missions

Medical missions trips require a highly specialized team; usually nurses, doctors, and paramedics are used for this type of trip. The advantage of this type of trip is that it is a perfect vehicle to get believers into a field where usually Christians would not be welcomed. A village populated by Hindus would probably not appreciate a team of open-air evangelists bringing a new religion to them, but the same town would certainly welcome a team of doctors offering free medical care, without much concern for their religious affiliation. The down side of these trips is that they get quite involved from a legal perspective. Doctors who are licensed to practice medicine in one country are not necessarily permitted to practice in another country. Medicine that is considered "over the counter" in one country may have stricter regulations to overcome in the mission field. There are also cultural considerations that may hinder medical assistance. Antiretroviral medication, for example, has been wasted in many parts of the world where wristwatches were not easily available. If the regiment is not taken at the right time with the correct regularity, the medication becomes ineffective.

There is a reason these excursions are usually handled by large, wealthy corporations, the military, or government-funded teams. International medical trips are complex and expensive. But they are also ideal opportunities to bring the gospel to meet the spiritual needs of people, while showing the love of Christ by taking care of their physical needs. Much wisdom needs to go into finding out what is legal, what licensing requirements there are, and what the customs regulations are about bringing in medicines. You wouldn't want your team arrested for drug smuggling.

Vacation Bible Schools

Vacation Bible Schools are events that churches offer to entertain, teach, and care for local children for, say, a week, in order to build relationships with the parents, impart the gospel to the children, and create awareness of the church's love for its community. The challenge with this effective ministry is that it requires a number of energetic, creative, and available volunteers. By not charging for the service, the number of children that will attend increases dramatically, but some churches lack the human resources to pull this off in the requisite daylight hours. A team of volunteers from the missionary's sending church can meet this need, and provide a dose of novelty that adds to the draw for the children. A VBS we ran in Japan was a colossal success because the parents wanted their children to practice their English on real, live English-speaking foreigners. The presence of an international group of workers helped increase the credibility of the church and fostered long-term relationships with parents, as children returned each year for the "Vacation Bible and English School."

Your church will have gifted and equipped people who are willing to spend their vacation time serving the Lord by teaching, evangelizing, or serving internationally. Start with evaluating who is willing to go, what their particular gifts are, and then go hunting for a place to put that dream team to work in the field. Of course, not just anyone who is willing and has a pulse is necessarily qualified to be on an STM team, which brings us to an important chapter.

6

THE DREAM TEAM:
SELECTING TRAVELERS

E mily Lazarus' poem *The New Colossus* has been immortalized by the
inscription on the Statue of Liberty. This iconic stanza that champions
the open arms of a free country is moving and inspirational:

> Give me your tired, your poor,
> Your huddled masses yearning to breathe free,
> The wretched refuse of your teeming shore.
> Send these, the homeless, tempest-tost to me,
> I lift my lamp beside the golden door!

What a magnificent sentiment! If you are ever tasked with starting a democracy, read those lines repeatedly for inspiration. But when inviting applicants for an STM team, you might want to be a tad more selective.

CREAM OF THE CROP VS. BOTTOM OF THE BARREL

Contrary to the common and disabling misconception, people do not volunteer for an STM trip. They apply. The team leader should not feel obligated to take everyone who puts up his or her hand. The purpose of the trip is to assist the missionary on the field. It is not a church-sponsored life-experience opportunity for sheltered teens. When a team consists of those who overestimate their abilities, those who are bored, those who want free travel, and those who are looking for a spiritual hit, the missionary is not helped, he is burdened.

There should be a sentiment in the church that we are sending the missionary our cream of the crop, not the bottom of the barrel. I have on occasion had to be frank with a missionary and tell him that the team we were able to assemble is one that may be a burden. I am very open about the team's strengths and weaknesses, and I always leave the missionary the option to pull the plug on the trip if he feels it won't meet his need.

Here are some factors to appraise when considering applicants for an STM trip.

First, *character* is far more important than skills and experience. Just as the qualifications for elders and deacons in the church are almost entirely spiritual traits, godliness goes a long way to make up for inexperience. A first-grade school trip to the museum is, for the teacher in charge, more about keeping the kids from breaking anything than about accomplishing their education of things prehistoric. In the same way, a team of immature believers will involve preventing them from doing long-term damage to the mission field.

When things fall apart, trust in God, patience, contentment, and submission will go a long way to helping any situation that crops up unexpectedly. Not everyone needs to be elder qualified, but if the team consists mostly of mature believers, the immaturity of young believers will be compensated.

Second, the *skills* needed for the job are important if the goal is to help the missionary, not hinder his work. A team of accountants, lawyers, and computer programmers will excel in the analytical and financial preparation of the trip, but the building they erect may end up being a death trap. Professionals are wonderful people I'm sure, they just aren't widely known for their brick masonry skills. If the missionary is counting on teaching to be done, then the team should have the requisite number of teachers. If he has asked the team to lead music while they are in town, the team needs to have a minstrel in their midst. This seems pretty simple, but I have been amazed by how many STM teams are assembled by simply asking for volunteers and then accepting everyone who raises their hand, with no thought of what the team needs to be able to *do* for the missionary.

Third, *travel experience* is helpful. Not everyone on the trip needs to have circumnavigated the globe to qualify, but a couple of globe-trotters in the mix will help the team leader greatly. The team leader may need to split the group into taxi-sized cohorts at some point. If someone has never negotiated with an Arab taxi driver before, the experience could be daunting. Your first trip into a territory where your mother tongue is not understood can be flustering. Something as simple as buying bottled water in India can reduce the uninitiated to tears. Experience breeds confidence, which has a much-needed calming effect in the face of unforeseen events abroad.

Foreigners have a persistent tendency do things in a way that is, um, foreign. They can make the inalienable right to relieve oneself such a traumatic affair that you vow never to use a bathroom again. On a trip to Egypt, a first-time traveler in our group emerged with his trousers drenched in water, much to the clamorous glee of local gawkers. My first foray into a Japanese bathroom left me in no wonder why the population is known for their intelligence. The toilet seat came with a complicated electronic console marked with glyphs and lights, and looked like a bachelor's degree was a prerequisite to operate it safely.

I once walked two miles in the blazing heat of an Israeli desert with a heavy backpack weighing me down, while hitchhiking unsuccessfully. As soon as I gave up walking and collapsed in exhaustion, a car stopped to offer me ride. Apparently backpackers in need of a ride in Israel—unlike those in my home country—always remain stationary. It was a valuable tidbit of data

I could have used before achieving dehydration. These types of lessons are only learned the hard way. To have a few intrepid world travelers on your team could spare you a lot of unwelcome "on the job" training.

THE MANY FACES OF EXPERIENCE

Don't you hate it when all the advertisements for the entry-level position you are hunting for read, "Must have two years of experience"? How are you supposed to *get* the experience when everyone wants people who already have experience? This is where internships, apprenticeships, and other training programs are helpful. Likewise, if you insist that everyone on your STM trip has STM experience, you effectively create an impenetrable standard that no new believer feels they can ever break into. Rather, it is wise to differentiate what type of experiences could contribute to a team dynamic. Even those who only have knowledge of tourist hotspots can be invaluable. You might not think of the elderly couple that spends every vacation on a cruise or package tour as having STM experience. But these folks understand the significance of paperwork, planning, punctuality, budgeting, following the leader's instructions, and even language barriers. They can be tasked with assisting in visa applications, ticket purchasing, itinerary arrangements, and other administrative issues.

A person who has no travel experience but is a gifted public speaker or enthusiastic evangelist, knows a smattering of the local language, or is a competent photographer, can greatly aid the team. Some people have an ability to be encouraging and cheerful in the midst of physical discomfort. Some have an uncanny sense of direction, or an intuitive ability to pick up on cultural nuances. These are all valuable assets that must not be overlooked by the one selecting the dream team. I'd take a team of cheerful, godly, patient, and submissive first-time travelers over the experienced globe-trotter who thinks he knows everything but gets frustrated with other team members and can't follow a simple instruction.

All that said, it is still important to have a spiritually mature team, and one that has at least some travel-savvy members. A good balance should be struck between the spiritually mature and experienced travelers making up the bulk of the team, a few inexperienced believers who are ready to be challenged sprinkled in the mix, and perhaps one or at the most two immature believers who need a wake-up call of how the world works. God can use an STM trip to yank the spiritually lethargic out of their comatose selfishness. They are being included for their benefit, not for the sake of the team or the ministry. But any more than one or two of these deadweights, and the team will suffer, which means the ministry will suffer. Misery loves company, and immaturity has a deleterious effect on team morale. As a rule I only allowed these problematic people on a team with a particularly strong team leader who possessed extraordinary shepherding skills. And I always warned him about my estimation of the potential problems, and offered him the right to veto their participation.

O CAPTAIN MY CAPTAIN: THE TEAM LEADER

The most important decision the church makes about the STM trip is who the team leader (TL) will be. The STM team is not a democracy; it is a benevolent dictatorship. The TL has supreme authority under God on the trip. The absolute worst possible turn of events for an STM team is if there is a mutiny on the trip. Not only does it disrupt the ministry, but also insubordination on the trip can devastate the witness of Christian love, unity, and submission that the missionary is trying to exemplify for those to whom he is ministering. A wise, patient, conscientious, reliable, experienced, confident team leader makes it easy for his team to follow him and trust his decisions.

The responsibility of instilling confidence in his leadership lies with the sending church leadership. The elders need to commission the team and specifically its leader publicly and unequivocally. The team needs to understand the protocol for objecting to the leader's decisions. If speaking to him privately bears no fruit, and the matter is not resolved satisfactorily at the posttrip debrief session, then the only recourse is to wait until the team returns home, at which point the matter can be dealt with by the church leaders. The missionary should not be burdened with shepherding relationship tension on the team, and under no circumstances should the local believers or unbelievers be exposed to the dirty laundry of intrateam disputes. This is not a junior-high field trip; it is a time to serve others by dying to self and focusing on the kingdom work at hand.

But the team leader needs to work hard to retain this confidence and be worthy of the authority given to him. The team leader's main role is to shepherd the team's relationship dynamics and organize (or delegate) the travel details and ministry objectives of the team. A disorganized team leader is a contradiction in terms. If you're disorganized, you're not leading the team. The team leader's job is basically to be an inspiring, omnicompetent travel agent, tour guide, nurse, counselor, secretary, project manager, music director, and all-round superhero. The TL is to the team what a soccer mom is to her family: everything.

Traits to look for in a TL: initiative, spirituality, decisiveness, ability to stay calm in crisis, evidence of wise stewardship of funds, travel experience is a must (preferably having been on an STM trip before).

LOCK DOWN TEAM PROFILE AND TRIP DATES

Ask the missionary about the size, age profile, skill requirements of the team, and the dates. Locking down dates is important, as it will be the first question people ask about when deciding whether or not to commit. They have work schedules to circumnavigate, family vacations booked, weddings to attend, and countless commitments that may or may not be able to be moved. The dates will make or break the decision for many would-be applicants. Nothing can be done until the missionary has the dates picked. At the very least lock down a range of dates; for example, "Two weeks between mid-June and mid-July."

THE INFORMATIONAL MEETING

The first step in picking a team is announcing an informational meeting for everyone who may be interested in the trip. A church leader should introduce the team leader, and then the team leader should take over the presentation of the trip.

At this meeting the team leader should provide the following details: the type of ministry, the destination of the trip, the estimated cost, and the exact dates (pending ticketing, which can shift the schedule by a day or two), and the deadline by which their application must be submitted.

This gives people all the information they need to make a considered decision to apply. The meeting must be sure to make clear that the next step is application, that spots are limited, and that not everyone who applies will necessarily be chosen. The criteria for acceptance should be mentioned, but leave enough leeway for the team leader's discretion.

THE APPLICATION FORM

The questionnaire is a tool that has many functions. It separates those who are really interested from those who are just curious. It weeds out those who are so hopelessly disorganized that they can't get the questionnaire in by the deadline. It also serves to send a clear message that they are applying to be considered for the trip, as opposed to signing up for a guaranteed spot on the team. It also forces them to notice the huge gaps in their résumé, which lowers expectations of being selected.

The purpose of the questionnaire from the perspective of the team leader who is selecting his team, is to ensure the skills needed are available and the level of spiritual maturity and experience is optimal, and it also lets him get a feel for what the dynamic of the trip will be like. For example, married couples come with their own issues (like insisting on sharing a room), and singles come with other challenges.

1. Please explain the circumstances of your conversion. This is not only to give the TL a sense of the person's understanding of conversion and potential maturity, but also their ability to articulate their testimony clearly—something every STMer should be prepared to do at the drop of a beret.

2. Are you a member of the church? It is natural to expect those who would represent the sending church to be official members of the church. It is essential to have everyone on the team subscribe to the theology taught by the sending church, and to acknowledge the sending elders as their spiritual leaders. I have found that STM trips are an effective catalyst to get fence sitters to commit to their church's membership process.

3. In what ministries or capacities do you currently serve? It is only reasonable to assume that a person applying to serve internationally is one who has evidenced a desire and faithfulness to serve locally. If this question is left blank, the team leader should respond to the applicant with an encouragement to obey the Scriptures' injunction to serve, with a view to applying for the next trip.

4. Please list your travel experience, including previous missions trips and any other international travel. As stated previously, this is not a requirement for every member of the team, but it is very helpful for the TL to select a team with the knowledge of who has what travel experience.

5. What special gifting, training, or experience do you possess that could benefit the team or the ministry (including languages you know, courses you have taken, qualifications you possess, and skills you have)?

6. What is your marital status or relationship status if unmarried? If the applicant is married, and the spouse has not applied for the trip, it would be wise to follow up with a question about the spouse's consent. A husband whose wife is feeling neglected by his constant business trips should not be applying for more time away from his family. Likewise a wife, who is applying for an STM trip against her husband's wishes, is not exemplifying the witness of a biblical marriage relationship. The STM trip should never be something that comes between marriages in the church. Question 20 is meant to help gather information about this sensitive factor.

7. What are your reasons for wanting to go on a short-term missions trip? This would prove to be a very revealing answer. Red flags include answers of this sort: "I've always wanted to travel, but couldn't afford it"; "I heard there would be godly girls on the team, and I want a missions-minded wife"; "My parents think it will make me more grateful." Commend these for their honesty, and then suggest they read this book to help get their motives right!

8. Do you have any health issues, including allergies? These may not preclude a person from eligibility, but some conditions may become a burden on the whole team, not just the individual. For example, meal times are not always easy to regulate on the field, and some conditions are aggravated by low blood sugar.

9. Do you have any dietary requirements or food allergies/aversions? The hosting church needs to be aware of food allergies before the trip so that, if the request is not a burden on the hosting church, they can make arrangements, and also to avoid offense when a person declines to eat what is offered. I include aversions to weed out any vegetarians or vegans. Some cultures would find it very cumbersome and confusing to have to accommodate a preference based on conscience about how animals are treated in the West, as many vegetarians do. If an applicant feels too strongly about their food preferences, or are limited by their allergies, depending on the field, they may need to recuse themselves from consideration.

10. Do you have any physical disabilities that the hosts would need to accommodate? I've sent teams with people who were deaf, or blind, or confined to a wheelchair, but only with the missionaries' assurance that the person could be accommodated without overburdening the receiving church.

11. Is there anything about your appearance that may be offensive in a foreign culture (e.g., tattoos, piercings, a man with long hair, unusually dyed hair color, etc.), and what do you intend to do about it (e.g., cover tattoos, remove piercings, cut hair)? These issues would not matter in some fields, but they should be run past the missionary for approval to be sure. And in any case, the question on what the applicant is willing to do about it reveals much about their attitude.

12. How do you intend to finance the trip expenses (personally, raising funds, a combination)?

13. If you plan to raise funds, how do you intend to do this?

14. Exactly how many weeks are you able to give to the trip itself (i.e., time off work)? Sometimes a trip is publicized as a three-week trip, but due to ticketing factors the trip runs twenty-two days instead of twenty-one. If this is cause for a person withdrawing, or getting into trouble at work, then it is best to know that before tickets are booked.

15. *Can you commit to a weekly team meeting on* _____ *at* _____ *until* _____? Having the answer to this question in writing will come in handy later when excuses are offered for missing mandatory team meetings.

16. *Can you commit to an overnight team service project on the weekend of* _____? Ditto.

17. *Are you willing to publicly share your testimony of conversion if called upon to do so?* Not everyone will need to do this, but a fair share of the team members will need to be able and willing to share their testimony, as speaking opportunities often present themselves without much warning.

18. *Do you commit to be present for the report to the sending church on* _____?

19. *Please ask the leader over the ministry you serve in at church to email a reference to the following address . . .* The reference will come directly to the team leader, not via the applicant. This takes pressure off the ministry leader from being tempted to just be positive, instead of being frank about the strengths and weaknesses of the applicant.

20. *Please ask your spouse (if married), or parents (if under 18) to email a paragraph of what they think of your desire to go on the trip, to the following address . . .* This is to help ascertain if the trip would cause problems in a marriage. In the case of children, it shows the applicant's parents the church's commitment to parental authority.

The completed application form must be received by the church office no later than _____.

Many who are curious about the trip may come to the introductory meeting, but fewer will follow through with the application form. Setting a deadline is important as it will help to reveal the applicant's ability to be organized and to show their seriousness about the trip. It also helps the TL stay on schedule with the organizational timeline he has set. The deadline should be reasonable though, and allow for the applicant to prayerfully consider their participation, their plan to finance the trip, and for them to ascertain how much leave they can take from work.

PRETRIP BONDING

Periodic meetings before the trip should be arranged to pray for the missionary, the trip's arrangements, and for the finances.

A hike or camping trip is an accelerated way to simulate discomfort and fatigue, which inevitably brings out the real character of people. This is not to cut people from the team, but to bring to their attention issues they need to work on and to be aware of while on the trip.

Another good bonding experience is to engage in some ministry activity similar to the one the team will be doing on the trip; for example, a two-day VBS, or a construction project at home for the sending church. The main thing the TL is looking for at this time is if there is anyone who is not submissive to his leadership or a threat to team unity.

7

THE BOTTOM LINE: IS IT WORTH THE MONEY?

In 1864 a young lady named Hetty Green received a bequeathal of $7.5 million and subsequently the unflattering sobriquet "The Witch of Wall Street." Not only would Hetty mysteriously fly over the penurious years following the Civil War, but she even managed to magically swell her fortune and gain notoriety as the first woman to make a splash in the masculine shark tank of the New York Stock Exchange.

Her magic formula was a simple brew of conservative stocks, Civil War bonds, a barrel of hoarded cash reserves, and a pinch of stinginess. Hetty Green embodied the epitome of frugality; to call her a miser would be, well . . . generous.

Hetty was so cheap that she eschewed the use of soap for washing her hands, and likewise instructed her laundress to only clean the dirtiest parts of her dress. She wore the same black frock until it was threadbare, drove an ancient carriage, and subsisted mostly on 15-cent pies. She once spent hours searching her carriage for a stamp worth 2 cents.

When her son broke his leg, Hetty took him to a free clinic for the poor, but when they refused admittance, she tried (free) home remedies. The boy lost his leg. Hetty herself suffered from a severe hernia, but refused to spend the $150 for her surgery.

Hetty Green died with a Zuckerbergian equivalent net worth of around $200 million (nearly $5 billion today). But she lived like a pauper, and gave nothing away. Ever.

Ned took his half of the inherited loot, and with prodigal efficiency, tried to roll Mama's corpse over in her grave. He shed cash like a deciduous money tree, spending Hetty's punctiliously pinched pennies on the most lavish extravagances, like a diamond-encrusted privy pot.

Hetty's daughter, Sylvia, on the other hand was known for her generosity. She gave to genuine needs, but managed to keep her entire fortune intact, eventually bequeathing it all to sixty-four churches, hospitals, and schools.

Looming over this story, like a told-you-so specter, is the parable of the rich fool (Luke 12:16–21). In it, Jesus warned against the soul-numbing tendency—instinctual in mice, magpies, and man—to hoard earthly treasures for themselves in lieu of spending it on work whose benefit will only be seen in the distant eternal future.

Deciding whether a particular STM trip is worth the cost is a complicated exercise. One has to consider fiscal factors as well as the eternal significance of the ministry, the intangible benefits of a visit, and the very real issue of whether the funds could be used more effectively in another ministry. So the stark reality is that STM teams need to justify their fiscal existence. Let us consider some of the factors that need to be weighed when deciding if a trip is necessary to accomplish the goal of holding the ropes. Sometimes sending the funds in a wire transfer may be the more efficient option. But then again, the need of the missionary and his ministry might require something far more valuable than money in the bank.

WHERE YOU PUT YOUR MONEY SAYS A LOT TO BELIEVERS

When a team from a well-known church or respected denomination arrives to come alongside a small, isolated church, the mere statement the trip makes can accomplish much good. The most financially costly trip I've ever taken was to a persecuted church in a closed country situated in the Himalayas. The journey took four days of travel, through five different airports, multiple nerve-racking bus rides, and all the expense that travel incurred. Once in the country, we drove for five hours at nauseating altitudes to meet twenty-two skittish believers in a forest. They were all intimately familiar with persecution. It was an honor to minister to them and be served a meal by them. I found out they had carried the pots full of food for a hike that took them five hours. They had left in the dark, freezing morning to be at this rendezvous point in time to prepare a clearing in the forest and make us a meal. You cannot put a price tag on some experiences.

The pastor of that church said that our visit to them was a message more encouraging than the sermon we preached. He said the fact that we were willing to come was saying to them, "You are important to us. We flew thousands of miles, and spent thousands of dollars, to be with you, to learn from you, to fellowship with you, and to help where we can. You are a significant member of the body of Christ, and we need you to be healthy."

Put that on your bottom line.

WHERE YOU PUT YOUR MONEY SAYS A LOT TO UNBELIEVERS

But it is not only believers who are affected by the trip. To outsiders you are declaring, "I'm not sure how many international visitors you normally receive, but this little group here has our attention, our affection, and our support. What they are busy with here is important enough to attract a team of foreigners every year. We value them more highly than the tourist sites you have to offer."

One Japanese pastor told us that his church had been considered a reason for shame in their neighborhood, until our team came from America to host an English Vacation Bible School. Over the years the church has built respect in the community by serving them with free English classes and daycare on an annual basis, which was not something the indigenous religious institutions had managed to do for them.

There are various species of missions committees. Each need has different concerns about the bottom line.

CHURCHES THAT SUPPORT MISSIONS RELUCTANTLY

One type of church is the one that is tightfisted and sees any money flowing out of the local region as better used where the results are visible. An extension on the children's building, a local soup kitchen for the poor, reupholstering the aging pews—these are needs right under our noses, so why go looking for needs abroad?

A common concern among those who guard the church's purse is that STM trips appear not to be a good stewardship of the church's finances. Most churches have limited resources. Every cent that goes to supporting an expensive international missions trip is one that does not go toward a plethora of biblically mandated local ministries. What assuages this concern is the understanding that STMs play an invaluable role in meeting the biblical responsibilities of other high-priority ministries.

Jesus left the apostles with a clear mission statement and a functional methodology: "You will be my witnesses in Jerusalem and in all Judea and Samaria, and to the end of the earth" (Acts 1:8). He told them to start in that city, and then move in concentric circles outward to the familiar culture and foreign culture of the local regions, and then progress on to the rest of the known world. What we today call "missions" is simply our generation's leg of the relay race to take the gospel to the ends of the earth. The STM trip is part of the support structure for that endeavor, arguably the most important task given to the church.

A local church that spends more money on its own sound system, air-conditioning, and gardens, than on supporting global missions, is a church that has not yet had Rockefeller's epiphany. It is a church that still thinks hoarding money for itself, instead of investing in eternity, will bring happiness and fulfillment. It is a church whose compass has been held too close to the world's magnetic field. When the direction is lost, the mission of the church is steered off course into self-focus, and then spending money on international missions seems out of place. But the mission endeavor, in all its forms, is the Dog Star of the local church by which we need to navigate our budgets. The end goal of more people worshipping Jesus rightly in the world is our guiding light. So, is sending a team of our people to support our missionaries worth the money? Only if your church is on course with the destination Jesus set for us two thousand years ago.

Another common concern is that if the church sends an STM trip in a tight financial year, then the budget will not be reached, because money that would normally go to the offering will instead go to the team. But this fear is unfounded and, dare I say, a misunderstanding of God's ability to provide and goodness to meet the needs of those in his service. The idea that an STM trip will ruin the church budget is simply unfounded. The trip is not being paid for out of the church coffers as a ministry expense, but rather out of the pockets of those individuals inside and outside the church who will donate specifically to the trip. Each traveler will send out support letters to people they know. Experience shows that the money that comes in for an STM trip is almost always donated by people who have a personal relationship with the individual travelers who are raising funds, or a vested interest in the ministry being done in a particular country.

In other words, if a potential donor knows and loves Joe or Sally, they will give money to support them. If Joe weren't going on a trip, the donor wouldn't think to give that money to the church instead. Or if Mrs. Donor "has a heart" for orphans, and hears that Sally STMer is going to work in an orphanage, Mrs. Donor will give over and above her normal giving to meet this need. If Sally never sent her a support letter, it's not as if Mrs. Donor would spontaneously donate over and above her regular giving to the church on the off chance that money makes its way to orphans.

The STMer will also send letters to acquaintances outside the church that would never give to the church normally. The acquaintance might be a rich aunt who attends another church, but wants to support her niece's interest in international missions. Or the donation might come from a coworker who doesn't attend church, but believes in what they deem "worthy causes."[10]

---

10 For a discussion on whether or not to accept funds from unbelievers, see chapter 8.

In fact, in my experience as an STM director and as a pastor who has access to the giving patterns of a congregation, I have found that in the year that an STM trip is sent, *more* money comes into the church per capita of membership than in years that no trip is sent. This makes sense on many levels. Not only are funds coming in from outside the church, and not only are donors inside the church giving over and above their regular giving, but the excitement and fulfillment of sending a team and then hearing their reports of God's work actually serves to mobilize people spiritually. They tend to have a more global, eternal mindset. And when people are thinking more biblically, and less selfishly, then they give *more* to the Lord's work, not less.

CHURCHES THAT LOVE LONG-TERM MISSIONARIES, BUT NOT STM TRIPS

Not all frugality is bad. It is a blessing when churches have wise stewards guarding the money like spiritual sentries. These churches are meeting the need to evangelize the globe, but they simply fail to see how STM trips are an efficient use of funds to accomplish that goal.

This type of church sees the STM trip as an exorbitant luxury to meet a need that could be handled with a cash donation made directly to the missionary. The other species of missions committee is one that is far too eager to fly over oceans and market an exotic adventure to meet a need that should be met with the boring but effective cash donation.

You may agree that in principle STM trips are a good use of money, but are they the *best* use of money? This question is more challenging to answer. If the trip is not meeting the biblical goal, or is poorly organized and misses its objective, then frankly, no, it is not the best use of money. Rather give the money directly to the missionary. You can hardly ever go wrong with that, assuming your missionary has integrity.

CHURCHES THAT ARE TOO EAGER TO FLY

Another type of church animal is the one that is too eager to fly. They love the hoopla and excitement of fund-raising and send-off services. They thrive on events and fund-raising barometers marking the rising level of cash to meet the well-marketed need. STMs are a dream come true in this environment. If a missionary shares in a prayer letter that they wish they could get a babysitter for date night, the church wants to mobilize a platoon of babysitters to cross eight time zones in order to meet that need. There is something to be commended in their zeal and compassion for their missionaries. But the bottom line will creak under the heavy burden of this type of frequent-flier syndrome.

Sometimes missionaries will request a team because it is the only way for them to get funds out of a stingy church. The church is looking for "what's in it for us?" So an exciting trip overseas is worth the fund-raising. If the missionary just requested cash for the project, he'd be faced with reluctance packaged in excuses, wrapped in red tape.

BUYING A SHARE IN THE COMPANY

Contributing cheerfully to the work of God in the world is a tangible and expedient way of participating in the family business. God's business is ruling and reigning and reaching out in spiritual expansion all over the world. God doesn't need our money, as if he lacks the resources himself—"The silver is mine, and the gold is mine, declares the LORD of hosts" (Haggai 2:8). God allows us to contribute so that we can enjoy the blessing of being part of his work, and so that we can reap the reward in this life and the next. "The point is this: whoever sows sparingly will also reap sparingly, and whoever sows bountifully will also reap bountifully. Each one must give as he has decided in his heart, not reluctantly or under compulsion, for God loves a cheerful giver" (2 Cor 9:6,7).

When nineteen-year-old Mark Zuckerberg approached his friend Joe Green to become a business partner of a nascent social networking company called The Facebook, Green declined. He feared raising his father's ire about hitching his career to the maverick teenage wunderkind who had recently been chastised by the Harvard disciplinary committee for sundry illicit programming shenanigans. The deal included a significant share in the company in exchange for Green's part-time commitment to help with programming and design.

Green later wryly called that decision his "billion dollar mistake."

With the 20/20 vision of hindsight, we know that anyone with the prescience to secure even a single share early on in a promising company like Facebook would not be second-guessing any sacrifice they endured to obtain that preternaturally profitable commodity. And yet any earthly dividend we could gain pales in comparison to the eternal weight of glory that awaits those who have sacrificed for God's kingdom enterprise. Many, however, demur on the decision and forego the coveted opportunity to be a part of God's expanding kingdom work.

When the "Particular Baptist Society for the Propagation of the Gospel among the Heathen" was formed on October 2, 1792, the inauspicious sum of 13£ 2s 6d was raised in the form of promissory notes (checks) and deposited into a snuffbox. The collection was meant to be the seed that would germinate into a fund to support a volunteer missionary to move abroad. The donations were the financial rope that the Society gripped, as William Carey descended into the dark pit of India.

It was an exciting prospect—to fund the first evangelistic venture of its sort in modern church memory. And those with eternal perspective saw it for what it was, a fortuitous opportunity to buy a share in the most profitable work imaginable—namely, investing in God's mission to save the lost.

One of the lowest amounts was promised by a young, penniless student named William Staughton. Determined not to let his impecunity rob him of the opportunity to become a founding member of the society, he borrowed the money and worked to pay it off.

Later he would say, "I rejoice over that half-guinea more than over all I have given my life besides." And for good reason—that sacrificial contribution assured young Staughton a mention in the annals of British history, a stake in the birth of world missions, and unimaginable return on investment in the form of eternal reward in heaven.

Jesus said, "And everyone who has left houses or brothers or sisters or father or mother or children or lands, for my name's sake, will receive a hundredfold and will inherit eternal life. But many who are first will be last, and the last first" (Matt 19:29,30).

To minister in the kingdom is both a privilege and a duty. Jesus commands his followers to invest in eternity, not hoard treasures on earth; sow bountifully into his kingdom work; and trust him to provide for their needs of food and clothing. God does not call his servants to act and then leave them destitute of the resources to obey. The determining question should be: "Is this STM a ministry we believe God wants us to do?" If so, do it. If the money does not come in, you will know the trip was never God's will. If it is God's will, then a little thing like cash and coin will not stand in his way.

Providing the money for ministry is God's prerogative; spending it wisely is ours. And that's the bottom line.

8

THAT MAKES CENTS:
HOW TO RAISE FUNDS
FOR STM TRIPS

Robert Kiyosaki, in his popular book on personal finances, *Rich Dad, Poor Dad*, recounts a humorous story of when he and his boyhood friends first decided to "make money." They collected the used lead toothpaste tubes from people in their neighborhood. They then melted the lead and poured them into plaster of Paris cast molds, making coins. Naturally, his parents soon informed him that "making money" in that way was illegal.

One of the most intimidating aspects of an STM trip is coming up with the money. But funding the travellers is an obvious and critical part of the STM trip. As William Carey averred in his "Enquiry" when exhorting his readers to give liberally to missions, "We must *plan* and *plod* as well as pray... Then we must *pay* as well as pray and plan."[11] This challenge, however, is not one the individual travelers need to bear alone. The church needs to take primary responsibility for financing those they send. There should be an expectation in churches that the STMers will be sending out letters to raise support for their trip.

Raising support is a biblical principle modeled in the New Testament. In 1 Corinthians 9, Paul makes the point regarding his own right to be supported in his ministry. Granted, in the context it is clear that Paul had forgone his right for the sake of not being accused of doing ministry for sordid gain by the unbelievers among whom he ministered, but he makes a sound argument that it is perfectly normal for ministers to expect support for the ones who do the work of the ministry, from those who benefit from the work of the ministry.

STEP ONE: SET A GOAL AMOUNT

Set a goal amount for the team, and divide by the number of individuals.

The goal amount is the sum total of all the costs the trip will incur, from airplane tickets to yellow-fever inoculation injections. It is essential to include all expenses. The key to a financially viable STM trip (and life!) is setting a comprehensive and realistic budget.

It helps the missionary to have a list of specific questions about the costs that the team anticipates incurring.

- What will it cost to rent a car, or will one be loaned to the team?
- What insurance is needed (travel, medical, car)?
- How much will the team need to pay for accommodations, meals, and transport contributions (gas money, tollgate fees, parking, etc.) to hosts?
- Are there any domestic flights and bus/train/subway rides that will increase the cost of transport? (Sometimes missionaries take for granted the cost of a daily return ticket on a subway, but

---

11 S. Pearce Carey, *William Carey*, 70.

a team of fifteen travelers, for two weeks, adds up quickly, and should be budgeted for beforehand.)

- Will the team need to provide the materials for a building project or VBS or other services?
- Will there be any theme park, game reserve, or other outing for which the team will need to pay an entrance fee?
- Is the team responsible to pay for the locals who accompany them to restaurants or other venues that incur costs?
- Will anyone on the team be required to acquire an international driver's license?
- What types of gifts and for whom would it be appropriate to bring gifts besides the missionary family (e.g., for the elders of the church, the host homes, an intern who will be doing the driving, etc.)?

There are also costs that the traveler will incur personally for which the team funds may be used to reimburse them. Some opt to leave these types of expenses up to individuals, but in that case it should be made clear before applications are accepted exactly which costs the team will be raising funds to cover. Some churches raise the airfare, in-country travel costs, meals, and accommodations. Other churches cover more or all costs related to the trip. This means that application for the trip is not limited to those who can afford it. The cost of paperwork and medical precautions can be prohibitive to some financially challenged people.

Also consider if the following costs will be paid for out of raised funds, or will be up to the individual's personal costs:

- Passport and visa application, expediting, and delivery costs, if applicable.
- Vaccinations.
- Region-specific medication, such as malaria pretreatment.
- Region-specific gear, such as sunblock, water purification tablets, mosquito nets.
- Stamps and stationery for support letters, in-country correspondence, including wi-fi expenses. For example, our

church required that each STMer send out one hundred, full-color support letters with preaddressed and stamped envelopes. But the church then also allowed those materials to be paid for out of the raised funds.

- If the team leaders are required to have international roaming capability on their cell phone, to whose account is that expense?

There are many other costs that you may think of specific to the type of trip or composition of team members, but these are a few of the basic ones. The thinking to avoid is, "These costs are so minor, it's easy for the individual to pay them." That may be true, but it might also be that many of these costs add up to become an unnecessary burden on the team members. On the other hand, if the team opts to cover all of the expenses for all the members, that will increase the goal amount so much that it may prove more daunting to raise the inflated target amount than to simply each carry a part of the burden personally.

STEP TWO: WRITE A SUPPORT LETTER

Support letters have proven to be simple and effective means of bringing in support for STMs. In his letter to the Romans, Paul included information about his desired trip to Spain and went as far as to say, "I hope to be helped there by you"!

Tax Deductibility

This is a tricky subject, not only because every country has different laws about this, but because of the obstacle it can be to giving. In general, tax deductions work like this. If a donor gives money to a nonprofit organization, like a church or a missions agency, they can report that on their tax returns, and perhaps benefit from it. In order for this to work, the STM trip needs to be 100 percent in line with the stated goals of the nonprofit organization. Also, it usually implies that money cannot be designated for an individual.

Safety in Numbers

A policy we employed at Grace Community Church worked well. We said that if any STMer sent out one hundred support letters and still came up short, the church would do its best to provide the difference. They had to provide a list of names and addresses they sent to in order to claim the prize. What happened in practice is that they then had the incentive and motivation to send all one hundred letters out, which inevitably brought in enough funds to cover their trip. Some fell slightly short, but others raised more than was needed for them, so there were plenty of funds for everyone. Some opted not to send all one hundred letters, but they then committed to pay in the difference themselves. Win-win.

Content of a Support Letter

When sending out a letter, include a description of the ministry, the authority it is being done under, and the goals. Also make sure there is a very clear and simple way to respond (i.e., provide banking details, or an address for a check to be sent to with a specific reference, etc.). Graciously mention the date by which the funds need to be in by, which helps people to plan their contribution and to remember to send it in.

Paragraph 1: personal information about how God called you to be part of this ministry. Each individual's letter will have a different opening paragraph.

Paragraph 2: ministry details. This paragraph explains what the team will be doing and how it fits in with the church's goals. Everyone on the team will have identical wording here, and it should be written by the team leader.

Paragraph 3: instructions on how to give financially, in wording provided by the team leader. This should include the church's electronic bank details and/or any directions about how the check should be filled out. This paragraph would be the one to contain information about tax deductions, if applicable.

Included in the letter should be a self-addressed, stamped envelope, as well as a photograph of the team or the missionary to which the team will be traveling. Under the typed copy of the letter, the team member should include a short handwritten note to personalize the letter for each recipient.

STEP THREE: CHOOSE YOUR SUPPORT BASE

There are three sources of funds: those in the sending church, the STMer's extended family in other churches, acquaintances, and family who are not believers.

Home Grown

The sending church needs to take responsibility for those they send. We ought not expect each individual STMer to act like a fund-raising Rambo, an army of one, to single-handedly assault the hordes of obstacles that stand between him and a successful mission. The trip is a church family affair. Even if a particular traveler has the financial wherewithal to finance his own trip, by inviting others into his ministry, the blessing is spread. It is an honor to serve the King abroad, but not everyone can go. Those who have to stay behind can be as much a part of the mission as the ones going. This is the beauty of the church-supported mission.

Blood Money: The STMer's Family

Blood runs thicker than water, or so the cliché goes. Aunts and uncles, grand-parents, and other possible familial patrons are a fertile source of funds. This can be an opportunity to bring your family into your ministry, and can be an exciting way for your relatives to be a part of your adventures. You should show discretion in which family members you intend to tap. Some, especially mature believers who are familiar with the STM process and benefits, will be delighted to assist. Others in the family may feel that it is inappropriate for relatives to solicit funds from within the family. Be sensitive about family norms, propriety, and politics.

Plunder the Egyptians: Outside Funds

One young man came to me in turmoil about not being able to send out sup-port letters to believers, because he simply did not know any believer outside of his own church. He was a fairly new believer, with only a few Christian friends. His whole family were not Christian. None of his school or work friends were believers. He wanted to use the trip as an opportunity to talk to his family and friends about Christ. He wanted to tell them what it was he would be doing on the trip and why he was driven to do this. His hope was that they would be challenged to consider their own lives, and to see how his formerly selfish existence was being transformed by the gospel—his priorities, his vacation time, his interests had been altered by an encounter with Christ.

So, what's the problem? Why the turmoil? Because someone had told him that God didn't want him to use money from unbelievers to do God's work.

On the other hand, someone else had pointed out to him that God commanded Moses and the fleeing Israelites to "plunder the Egyptians" from whom they were escaping (Ex 3:22). God funded the nation of Israel's journey with livestock, gold, jewels, and other valuables belonging to pagans. And the houses they were to occupy in the Promised Land had been built and furnished and developed by the pagan Canaanites.

Both those approaches are simplistic and unhelpful. God's command to Moses was not to "fund" anything. It was a judgment on the Egyptians for their four hundred years of oppression. God provided miraculously for the needs of the Israelites and punished the Canaanites for their idolatry. But to say that we can never use money offered by unbelievers to do God's work is also a bit naïve. A government tax break for nonprofit organizations—which most churches accept with relish—is another way of accepting financial benefit from a secular institution, populated by unbelievers. The money in the church offering that comes from believers' pockets was earned selling goods and providing services to unbelievers. Also, all the money in the world is God's anyway; so whether it comes through an unbeliever, or a fish's mouth, or a believer who got it from an unbeliever, are all irrelevant factors. God moves the heart of people to give, so that he can use the money for whatever he wants.

Though some object stringently to accepting cash from unbelievers, using fund-raising activities where unbelievers will contribute (e.g., car washes), these events create awareness in the community of a vibrant, missions-minded work of God in their midst. They can be used as a platform to share the gospel, invite people to church, explain the purpose of the missions trip, and all the while build team unity and raise funds for the work.

Ultimately the decision to accept money from unbelievers is a matter of the individual's conscience, and should be considered under the guidance of the sending church's leadership. If the church is going to make a policy about the team not being allowed to solicit funds from outside the church, then the church must bear the financial responsibility of making up the shortfall of the individuals, especially those who are new believers or new to the church.

STEP FOUR: MONITOR SUPPORT LEVEL UNTIL A CRITICAL MASS IS REACHED

After the letters are sent, money will begin to trickle and then gush in. But if the trip is simply overambitious and therefore unreasonably expensive, or there are too many people traveling, or if the congregation has been too burdened by other special appeals that year (e.g., building projects, new staff members' salaries, other STM trips), then the amount that comes in might not be enough to make the trip viable.

How does one determine this? With a crystal ball. Just kidding. There is no way to predict with certainty if all the money will come in or not. The best one can do is to only spend money that has already come in. Never go into debt presuming that funds will come in. Practically, this means that you will determine what your most crucial large expense is (almost always travel costs, and specifically plane tickets), and only when that amount is achieved is the trip deemed viable. One trick is to place a deposit on the tickets when enough has come in to do this. That way if the trip gets canceled, there is no debt, and the full amount has not been lost, only the deposit.

The next threshold is when enough has come in to pay the balance of the ticketing cost. What the team leader should be monitoring is the overall amount and which individual team members are responsible for bringing it in. If there is an individual who is lagging way behind everyone else, they could be called in for a shepherding moment. They can be asked if their letters have all been mailed yet, or if they have a secret plan to pay for the ticket themselves. Some will also bring in more than their share. This can offset others who are behind in their goals. If the overall amount is enough, the team leader may choose to overlook those who are underperforming. This is the nature of team fund-raising. If the reason for underperformance is a bad attitude, laziness, or a presumption that others will cover the shortfall, then that problem should be dealt with from a spiritual angle, not a financial one.

STEP FIVE: BUY TICKETS OR MAKE FURTHER APPEALS AND CUT BALLAST

If enough comes in to buy tickets, this should be executed as soon as possible, as many airlines give better rates for early ticketing. If, however, the clock is ticking and funds are not forthcoming, the trip is in danger of being canceled. The team should be rallied for an all-out attempt to raise funds, including team projects like car washes. If these attempts fail, or are obviously not going to be enough to make a difference, then a last resort is to ask the church leadership to make an appeal on behalf of the team.

There comes a time when a person has not raised enough to meet the need. At this point the team leader needs to decide if the reason is their negligence or not. He also needs to determine if there is enough other money that has come in to cover the costs of the team as a whole. He also needs to weigh up how important this person's role is and what cutting a member would do to the morale of the team as well as the effectiveness of the ministry. That judgment call must be made with much wisdom.

The team leader's options are: exhort the member to try harder, mobilize the whole team to help that person raise his portion, ask the church to subsidize him, or as a last resort cut him from the team for evidencing a lack of commitment to the trip (if this is true).

In some cases a person may have done everything required of them, and done so with gusto, and still come up very short. This type of team member should not be cut, but should be helped by the team. I once informed a team leader that I believed it was time to cut someone who had raised absolutely nothing. The team leader interceded for the person, vouching that they had exhibited great commitment and competence but simply did not know many people who had money to spare. I agreed fully that we should rather subsidize this person from the surplus of other teams we had at our disposal. I have, however, asked people to recuse themselves from the team when they have displayed bad attitudes about the fund-raising process.

Ships can have a certain amount of deadweight on board. But when the ship starts sinking and weight needs to be reduced to keep the cargo and crew afloat, it is the ballast that gets tossed overboard. This may seem harsh to think of team members as deadweight, but if one person is jeopardizing the entire ministry because of their negligence or sin, then they need to be removed to keep the ministry afloat. Even Jonah understood that!

STEP SIX: BUY TICKETS OR ABORT MISSION

If after a last-ditch, all-out campaign to raise the needed amount fails, then the trip must be canceled. This is a difficult and deflating turn of events, but it is better than going on the trip anyway, and presuming on others to bail you out. In my experience the absolute worst time to ever try raising funds is after the trip has returned. People do not easily give money for goals that have already been accomplished. Some may call it "stepping out in faith," others may call it "presuming on God's grace." The step of faith is made when the letters go out. The faith is this: if God wants the trip to go, he will provide the funds to do so. Conversely, if the funds do not come in, that should be taken as a providential intervention from God to stop the trip.

If the final resort worked and the money has come in, then tickets can be purchased, even if there is a small shortfall. Once the tickets are bought, there tends to be a renewed vigor to make the trip work. It's like the boys who encountered an insurmountable wall between them and their desired playground. They threw their caps over the wall and said, "Now we have to find a way to get over that wall!"

STEP SEVEN: HOLD FUNDRAISERS AS A TEAM TO MAKE UP ANY SHORTFALL

Once the tickets are purchased (or whatever the big make-or-break expense is), the shortfall can be tackled by encouraging the individuals who are low to work harder at achieving their goal, or the team could band together to do events that would bring in money. The team should not be segregated into those who still need to raise money and those who have done their share. In fact, it is a good practice to not tell the team who is short, but rather only inform individuals of their personal support level, asking them to keep it private. Otherwise there may develop an attitude of "Why should I wash cars, when it's Joe who is the one who is short?" A team mentality should be maintained at all times.[12]

SPENDING IN-COUNTRY

Keep every receipt for every expense. Always try to cover the missionary's personal expenses (e.g., lunches), and the expenses he incurs due to the team (e.g., tollgates, parking). You should also leave him with a cash amount that would cover the increased expenses of groceries, electricity, water, fuel, heating, or whatever the team added to the burden of the missionary family. Host homes should be treated the same way.

One way to administer the funds is to give each traveler a *per diem* amount of cash. This is an allotment per day, which must be used to pay for food, transport, accommodations, etc. The advantage of this is that the cash is spread over multiple people, so the security risk of being robbed is low. It also means that if you get hopelessly lost, you have some resources to get to your next destination. This system has the great benefit of not needing a receipt for every item. It cuts down on the accounting and paperwork. The disadvantage is that logistically it becomes problematic to have each traveler stand in line to purchase their train ticket and to pay for their meal separately.

Another method that some teams prefer is to have the team leader hold all the cash and then pay for everything. If individuals incur costs, they need to present a receipt in order to be reimbursed by the team leader. The advantage is that tickets, accommodations, and meals can be paid for in bulk. It is just more paperwork. The security risk can be mitigated by assigning amounts of cash to be carried by individuals in sealed envelopes. Then, as the team leader requires the cash, each member yields his or her stash in turn. As long as no one uses the cash without the team leader's permission, this system effectively guards against theft.

---

12 The team mentality is not only good for morale, but it is legally required by the tax requirements of many countries. For tax-deductible trips, money cannot be given to individuals but must be given to the team. A team leader cannot cut a person from the team for not receiving adequate funds; he can only be cut for lack of commitment to the team's goals, which may be evidenced by a lack of raising support.

9

ROUND TRIP:
TRAVEL AND CULTURE SHOCK

The famous escape artist, Harry Houdini, was a master showman who started his dazzling career as really little more than a glorified locksmith. The art he perfected was staging circumstances with lethal consequences, from which he would then escape with death-defying dexterity. The more inescapable the incarceration seemed, and the more perilous the consequence, the more satisfyingly miraculous the escape would appear. Throughout his illustrious career, his stunts became increasingly impressive. One act began as an escape from a giant milk can and evolved into one of his more spectacular demonstrations: the cuffed and shackled Houdini was stuffed inside the man-sized milk can, which was then enclosed in a nailed and chained wooden crate, and dramatically dropped into a river with two thousand pounds of lead attached to it. In less than a minute the nonplussed artist would emerge unshackled from the water, while the box would be hoisted by a crane and found to be unbroken, still locked shut, with the leg-irons left inside.

Houdini was not, however, invincible.

One of his claims was that he could endure any blow to the stomach, no matter how hard. He regularly challenged professional boxers to punch him in the gut, as he stoically and unflinchingly absorbed the blow. But on October 31, 1926, after a tiring show, Houdini was reclining in his dressing room when a university student asked him if it was true he could withstand any blow. He casually affirmed the claim, and the young man suddenly hit the unsuspecting Houdini in the stomach several times at full force. Without the chance to prepare for the impact, the great Houdini was rendered as vulnerable as a turtle on its back. The trauma burst his appendix, and he died.

The success of an STM trip may hinge on the time the team had to prepare. The quality and quantity of training the team received before leaving is as critical to the effectiveness of the trip as the ministry done while in the field.

The chain of command, the priority of godly responses, and the focus on dying to self are all spiritual paradigms that you don't turn on by flipping a switch. They take practice and commitment. Selecting, obtaining, and packing the correct clothing, luggage, equipment, teaching materials, and other tools are not issues you want to be thinking about once you are in the field. They need to be handled in the preparation phase. This chapter will handle some of the loose ends you may want to think through before your trip. But first I want to mention a part of the preparation that is as vital to the trip's success as the travel arrangements—namely, spiritual preparation. Bracing yourself for a physically, emotionally, and spiritually difficult time, in which you will need God's special grace, will help you be ready for the impact of otherwise unanticipated trials that will punch you in the gut.

SPIRITUAL CARBO-LOADING

The STM trip is such a potent shot of spiritual adrenalin that the testimonies of those returning often sound like an overzealous infomercial for how life changing the trip will be. This may lead those who are waning in their zeal for the work of the Lord to think that going on this type of life-changing trip will make them more godly. Perhaps your spiritual walk with the Lord has slowed to a lethargic amble, or maybe your quiet time feels like a car that is puttering along haltingly in need of a tune-up. You see the STM trip as the spiritual recharging station.

In many cases the trip might be an event that escalates the seriousness about your faith like a quickened pulse, but that is not the reason we go on STM trips. I always told our STMers that the trip is not the time to *get* godly but to *be* godly. All STM trips are fraught with trip wires to your godliness. You need to be on the alert, prepared for every temptation that might entangle you and trip up the ministry. If you find yourself cruising blithely on a plateau of apathy, the solution is to prepare your heart for the trip. You could memorize verses about dying to self and serving others. You should be in prayer for your own soul as well as for the other team members and those you will encounter in the field.

The church I serve in sits precisely on the route of the world's most prestigious ultramarathon, the Comrades Marathon. Several members of our congregation have successfully completed the ninety-two-km race within the ten-hour time limit. Besides the gruesome details they share with me about how the race affects the body (loss of toenails is the first one that comes to mind), they also share their secrets of preparation for going the distance. Any endurance athlete knows the importance of "carbo-loading." This is when you eat copious quantities of complex carbohydrates, which take time to digest and release energy in a constant stream for several hours. The key to this tactic is to eat it the evening before, and never the morning of the race. Can you imagine starting a race at sunrise having just scarfed down a massive bowl of spaghetti?

In the same way, trying to read and study your Bible on the STM trip, in order to heighten your spiritual experience or infuse your days with God-centeredness, betrays naïveté. The STM trip will have a dense schedule of work and service to do. It will involve pouring out your knowledge, practicing your patience and selflessness, and it will leave you exhausted at the end of each day. Believe it or not, you might not even get time to crack open your Bible, and that's OK. People who obsess about having regular daily devotions on the trip are like people eating their carbohydrates while on the run. The trip is not the time for you to be working on becoming godly through spiritual disciplines; it is the race. Yes, the Comrades Marathon contributes to one's fitness, but it is not why you run the race. Your year of preparation to get fit is so that you can perform well on race day. The STM trip is the time to put into practice that for which you have been preparing.

THE HAZARDS OF TIME TRAVEL

Time zones are like latent parasites that you pick up hourly in the plane. The more of these time-nudging barriers you violate, the more destabilized your sleep pattern will feel the first few nights of attempted rest. Everyone's body has a different way of protesting to sleep disruption, but in general it is advisable to force yourself to keep your ideal routine as soon as possible. So, if you want to be sleeping at 10 p.m. and awake at 6 a.m., then your first night back you should not retire more than an hour or so earlier, nor should you succumb to the temptation to sleep too late the next day. It can feel unnecessarily ascetic, but the sooner you need to get into a routine, the more brutal you need to be with your body the first three days back.

There may be other reacclimatizing that needs to happen. The disparities between where you have been the last few weeks and where you now need to function can make you feel like a scuba diver in a hot-air balloon. Sudden changes in temperature, humidity, diet, and even air pressure can hit you over the head with nausea, vertigo, constipation, and insomnia. Medication may relieve some symptoms, but there is no substitute for stalwart perseverance. Just get on with life, and your body will catch up.

SPEEKA DA ENGLEESH

One presumptuous mistake English speakers tend to make is assuming that the rest of the world is conversant enough to meet your most basic needs. That's not too much to ask, is it—that the foreigners learn a smidgen of English to make our lives easier? First, they aren't foreigners; you are the foreigner. Second, you are visiting them, so the courtesy of basic vocabulary acquisition lies with the guest. (In fact, except for the believers who have invited your team, the rest of their compatriots may not view you a guest, but as an intruder.)

If you become frustrated that no one knows the word "bathroom" (because their teacher taught them "toilet") or "sparkling water" (because they say "fizzy"), then your demeanor may convey a condescending attitude you don't intend to convey. Learn basic greetings, questions, and compliments. And always start speaking their language as a sign of respect, before you do what English speakers are globally notorious for: expecting others to accommodate us.

CROSS YOUR HEART: DON'T MAKE PROMISES

Emotions may be heightened while you are there. You may feel tempted to make a promise to return, or to keep in touch, or to send a recipe or a book you mentioned in conversation, or whatever. People may hang desperately to those promises. "Hope deferred makes the heart sick" (Prov 13:12). It is best to avoid making any promises at all. Just surprise them with the recipe or by befriending them on Facebook. If you do catch yourself making a promise to someone, be sure to write it down and make a note to follow through with that promise. Make this an order of first priority upon your return.

BEARING GIFTS, WE TRAVEL SO FAR

Just like the three wise men who came bearing gifts for the newborn Jesus, well-chosen "gifts from afar" can be a significant statement of respect. Don't be insulting, like bringing soap. It could easily be seen as condescending to bring a gift that you mistakenly assumed was something your host does not have access to. When I lived abroad and people found out I was South African and assumed that implied I lived in a mud hut, they would ask the most amusing questions. "Do you have calculators? Do you have chocolate? Do you have iPods?" I would sometimes hear my facetious inner voice tempting me to reply either, "What is a cal-koo-late-tor?" or more sarcastically, "Indeed we do, and we also have electricity, indoor plumbing, oh, and a space program." But instead I would just explain that as a British colony our country was blessed with the education, culture, and technology that most Western countries enjoy.

It is best to give gifts that can definitely not be found in their country because they are distinctly exotic. If you can't restrain yourself from giving soap or a calculator, be sure they are inscribed with your country's flag or some other unique local flavor, which is the real gift. Or if your country is known for a particular product, these can be good gifts—for example, Belgian chocolate, Swiss Army knife, or Statue of Liberty keychain (since you can't smuggle in an American apple pie).

Also, when you purchase souvenirs to take back to your family and friends, bear in mind that your spending will leave an impression on your hosts. An STM trip is not a shopping spree; it's a missions trip. Your goal is not to make a deal, plunder loot, and make off with underpriced swag. Your goal is to witness, encourage, and edify. Buy enough to show interest and appreciation for your host's culture, but not so much cargo that they are left thinking you came to take advantage of their weaker currency in order to stock your personal import/export company.

FLIRT ON THE FLIGHT BACK

The playful injunction, "Flirt on the flight back," puts a positive spin on a serious prohibition, "Never flirt on an STM trip." This was a facetious little policy I issued when I trained dozens of single college students. Unless you are married, or God has granted you the gift of singleness, you may unexpectedly discover a worthwhile distraction while preparing for the STM trip: the opposite sex.

And of course, there is nothing inherently pernicious about that. I would counsel any Christian young adult who is looking for a potential marriage partner that the best place to find someone who is godly, servant hearted, and ministry minded, is by looking around while serving in the ministry of God. While you are engaged in the Lord's work, simply pause and notice who is laboring alongside you, and you may discover someone who is suitable with which to pursue a deeper relationship. But . . . and it's a big "but" . . . the STM trip is not the right place to do anything about that discovery.

Singles who flirt with, or otherwise express romantic interest in each other, tend to be—bless their hearts—distracted. This is not necessarily sinful, nor inappropriate even, unless the forum for this cloud-nine dizziness happens to be an STM trip that is meant to be focused on serving others.

I told the single people in our STM training seminars, "By all means observe each other in ministry, notice each other's strengths and weaknesses, but for the sake of all things good and pure, only start to flirt on the flight back!" That usually evoked a nervous giggle or two, but the point is a serious one. Once the ministry objectives have been accomplished—which is approximately the same time that you are crammed back in economy class to home—you can begin to pursue other objectives again; getting married, for instance.

ALIEN ENCOUNTERS: REPRESENTING YOUR COUNTRY

It is fine to be patriotic to a certain degree. It is wholesome for people to love their countries and express that sentiment. The one place your patriotism will lose its charm, though, is anywhere outside the borders of your beloved country. I once attended a baseball game at Yankee Stadium. I noticed a lone supporter of the opposing team sitting in the eye of a hurricane of dedicated Yankee fans (is there another kind of Yankee fan?). I also noticed that he kept a neutral jacket on over his team's T-shirt, and had his team's cap tucked in his jacket pocket. He reservedly celebrated his team's occasional successes with carefully restrained satisfaction. Was he being disloyal to his team? Of course not. He had followed them to New York City to spectate their game. And he wasn't wearing the enemy pinstripes. But he had enough sage diplomacy (self-preservation?) to not rub it in the faces of the host fans.

When you visit another country, and then fawn about how great your homeland is, you run the risk of inciting resentment or even envy. It is not charming for a visitor from an economically stable, politically free, superpower country to comment on how much they admire the scenery back home, miss their favorite ketchup brand, or appreciate their free media. This is tantamount to you visiting an orphanage and then telling the needy children how fantastic your parents are for spoiling you with luxurious Christmas presents every year—not appropriate.

On the other side of the spectrum, it is just as awkward for a visitor to be cynical about their homeland. If you badmouth your government and decry the opulence of your own society, you may think you are endearing yourself to those less privileged, but in reality you could be tainting your witness. Believers who survive in a persecuted environment tend to take very seriously the Scriptures that command submission to government and honoring one's leaders. They have been forced to wrestle with the tension between recognizing their government's shortcomings and yet the biblical mandate to respect those ungodly governments. When visitors come from a political system that is far more conducive to the spread of the gospel, and then those same visitors slander their governments, it is confusing and even offensive.

The best counsel for international ministry is to avoid discussing politics completely. If asked about your country or what you think of theirs, present your answers from a biblical perspective with cautiously vague language. Sometimes someone is persistent and it would be rude to avoid answering the questions—for example, if over dinner your host is asking and simply won't let the topic go. For such a scenario, craft an answer that acknowledges their viewpoints as valid but draws attention to the biblical perspective. Perhaps, "I appreciate my homeland as much as you do yours; I recognize our government has strengths and weaknesses like any government does; I'm so thankful I am a citizen of heaven and know that God is in control of everything that happens in the world. Please pass the salt," and then take a large mouthful of food that will keep you silent for a few minutes.

FOOD FOR THOUGHT

Some people have very unusual cravings. Medical books refer to this condition as *pica*; i.e., cravings for nonfood items. I once viewed a documentary about a lady who liked to eat cigarette ash. She would sprinkle it on her ice cream or mix it into her coffee. I've heard of pregnancy cravings for paint chips, cigarette butts, dirt, and rubber. Presumably, though, these eccentric folk would not find it malapropos if their dinner guests declined a side of ash with their dessert. However, host homes that have gone out of their way to provide an authentic local dish for their STM guests might not take it so lightly to see their efforts so unappreciated.

The STM trip is an opportune time for gastronomic adventure—not only because it takes advantage of the *esprit du place*, but chiefly because it helps to accomplish the STM trip's goals. If Christians selected a mission field based on the food they would be served, the most reached country in the world would be Italy. But what compels believers to take the gospel abroad is not our affinity for a particular culinary delight, but rather the understanding we have that "man shall not live by bread alone, but by every word that comes from the mouth of God" (Matt 4:4).

Dinnertime has a long and lascivious history of offending religious sensibilities. In 1 Corinthians 14 Paul preempted a brewing food fight over the meat offered to idols. He also had to explicitly inform the Colossians to "let no one pass judgement on you in questions of food and drink" (Col 2:16). Later Paul warned Timothy that false teachers would teach that certain foods should be avoided.

Never curl up your nose at a pungent smell. For the same reason you don't look down when you are traversing a treacherous swinging bridge, the sage STMer should resist the temptation to ask what the meal consists of, until after it has all been successfully swallowed. The team could rehearse its stoicism before the trip by preparing some fun, visually assaulting dishes for one another.

Teamwork is a good strategy where possible. On a trip to Japan the more adventurous of the team expressed their appreciation for the blubbery substance that they saw their more timorous teammates struggling with. The team eagerly swapped and shared portions with such dizzying efficiency that the host was blissfully ignorant of the sleight of hand at play. All the plates were satisfyingly empty by the end of the meal, though some would later have their valor applauded for "taking one for the team."

Of course, there are acceptable reasons for abstaining from the food offered at the table. There's no need for a lethal nut allergy to curtail a successful STM trip. But never just leave food uneaten. If you suffer from serious food allergies, do your homework to learn a polite phrase or two in their language to explain that your pickiness is biologically induced. Allergies should be announced before the meal is served, preferably through a tactful interpreter, and never after you've tasted a dish.

You may have grown up in the customer-is-always-right world of customizable menus. It may be perfectly normal for an American to ask the waiter to "hold the mayo, place the mushrooms on the side, and 'sub' the cheddar for mozzarella." But in many restaurants in the world this tampering with the menu is seen as rude and ungrateful, or insulting to the chef.

If your hosts are gracious enough to take you out to a restaurant, and if they ask you where you would like to eat, resist the urge to ask for McDonald's, or any other nonindigenous offering. Ask for something authentic, or better yet, leave the decision up to them.

THE PRICE YOU PAY: BRIBERY

You need to formulate your view of bribery before you embark on international travel. God strictly prohibits Christians from perverting justice by asking for a bribe or offering one in order to circumvent an unfavorable outcome.

"Whoever is greedy for unjust gain troubles his own household, but he who hates bribes will live" (Prov 15:27).

"The wicked accepts a bribe in secret to pervert the ways of justice" (Prov 17:23).

"By justice a king builds up the land, but he who exacts gifts [bribes] tears it down" (Prov 29:4).

"Surely oppression drives the wise into madness, and a bribe corrupts the heart" (Eccl 7:7).

Sadly, there are many societies in the world where bribery is a matter of course. When Christians travel, they are often confronted with corrupt officials who try to exploit them and exact a bribe. It is important to understand what bribery is, according to the Scriptures, so that your conscience is informed by God's Word, not your misunderstanding of terms.

Some of what we inaccurately call bribery in English is actually exploitation. For example, when a customs official confiscates your team's luggage, and offers to return it for a fee, that is not bribery, that is exploitation. This is not you trying to subvert justice, you are being robbed. Someone in power is abusing his or her position of authority to steal money from you. You are the victim here, and not the perpetrator. This situation is akin to a mugger in a dark alley that holds you up at gunpoint and offers to let you go if you give them your wallet. Your reaction would probably not be, "Sorry sir, my religion forbids me from offering you a bribe or being complicit in injustice. You will need to forcibly remove the wallet from me while I actively resist you." No reasonable observer would conclude that you were a willing participant in that crime. It is not a bribe; it is robbery. And a person in authority who exacts money from the innocent is robbing them.

On the other hand, if a customs official confiscated a Bible found in your luggage because it is against the law to bring Bibles into the country, then he is not victimizing you. You are at fault. To give him cash to overlook the law that you have broken would constitute a gross violation of God's Word. You would be guilty of bribery as it would be a willing participation in an injustice.

These matters can be complex. If you will be traveling to a country where exploitation and bribery are rife, you should discuss as a team before the trip what each person's conscience understands as violating God's Word. No one should ever act against their conscience. But once on the field, the decision made by a team leader is final, and any objections should be handled at the debrief session before returning, or if necessary with the elders upon the team's return.

BOOK OF LIFE

A passport is a document your government issues you in order to verify your identity and citizenship for use when you travel internationally. Your passport allows you to reenter your country, it allows you access to your country's embassy or consulate abroad. These privileges are often taken for granted until you lose your passport while out of your country. Suddenly the world becomes a very inhospitable place. Your country will not allow you back into their borders, so you will not be permitted to board a plane or boat heading to your homeland. Your embassy will view you as a potential threat, and will treat you as if you are lying about your citizenship. In short, your passport is your book of life.

Your passport is your most valuable possession once you leave your homeland. If you have to choose between losing all your luggage, money, camera, jewelry, and tickets, or losing your passport, you should have the presence of mind to consider everything you have to be rubbish, compared to the surpassing value of your passport.

I cannot stress this enough. The entire STM trip can grind to a bumpy and hostile halt if one member misplaces his or her passport. In a sense a team of twelve travelers should be viewed as a party of twenty-four entities, with each passport being accounted for as fastidiously as each warm body is. If all twelve people are there but only eleven passports, then the team's mission can be completely derailed until the passport is recovered. No more borders can be crossed, no more business can be attended to. It is a big deal.

In order to minimize the potentially disastrous fallout of a lost passport, each traveler should have a copy of the relevant pages (cover, picture, visas) in his or her luggage, and another copy in the luggage of another traveler. These copies help the embassy a lot in being able to quickly verify if you are who you claim to be. This moves you out of the ice-cold category of "potential threat to homeland security" into the warmly welcome zone of a "citizen in distress."

LOST AND FOUND

One of the most terrifying experiences for first-time travelers is to get lost in a foreign country. This can happen in the matter of seconds. As the team gets onto a train and one person boards the wrong carriage, panic can set in and fuel unhelpful behavior.

The team leader needs to give clear instructions that everyone knows in the case of getting lost. An example of the procedure is: If you get separated from the group on a moving train, spend a few minutes trying to locate them, but if that fails, get off at the next stop, wait for an hour, and then go back to the last place you were all together. This gives the team leader time to come find you, but allows for the contingency that the team only discovers you are missing after several stops. If you get lost in a busy metropolitan area, get back to the place you last were with the team if possible; if you are too lost to do that, then just stay where you are for six hours, to give the team time to look for you. After six hours, go to the nearest police station, leave a message there in case your team comes looking for you there, and check into a hotel, and check with the police station daily to see if anyone has come looking for you. If you have no contact with your team for three days, make your way to the embassy. The embassy is the safest place to wait.

Usually, having this type of practical talk with the team is enough to ensure that everyone listens carefully to the instructions of the team leader when on the field.

LOVE LANGUAGES

Since the debacle at Babel, language has been the biggest obstacle for international travel. It is helpful to learn a few phrases in the language you will be encountering. It is usually enough to master a few simple greetings, the words for "please" and "thank you," basic directions, numbers, and the name of your country of citizenship.

Gestures and other nonverbal cues can be the source of great comedy and consternation. It is worth finding out about any particular gesticulation to avoid or to recognize. If you neglect this preparation, you may end up trying to hail a taxi while inadvertently starting a fight.

10

HOMEWARD BOUND: REENTRY AND FOLLOW-THROUGH

George Mallory may well have been the first person ever to stand on the summit of Mount Everest. The reason we'll never know is—he never came back. Mallory's own grandson, who successfully summited in order to get closure for the unfinished family business, recognized the importance of a fully executed finish. He conceded that even if his grandfather had made it to the top, Sir Edmund Hillary still rightfully earned the moniker as the first man to conquer Everest, because he was the first to return with the report of success. Climbing up a mountain is only half the journey. Likewise your STM trip is not over until you have successfully returned. What constitutes a successful return? There is far more to your reentry than simply disembarking on home soil, uploading pictures to Facebook, and dishing out souvenirs to your supporters. Reentry is a physical, emotional, and spiritual challenge. What helps this process is a wise team leader and his most important posttrip responsibility: the team debrief session.

THE DEBRIEF

The team needs to remain focused on the ministry at hand while they are in-country. But people are sinners, and there will be interpersonal issues that arise. For example, personality conflict, tensions, annoyances, rivalries, romantic interests, and other occupational hazards of being human. Also, doctrinal differences with the host church might come to the fore, or a differing philosophy of ministry or style of musical worship. The team will amass questions, disagreements, concerns, or they may even want to offer advice or teaching. These issues can risk the unity of the team, the relationship with the host church, or in other ways become a distraction from the work the team has come to do. So in order to accomplish the team's goals, the time and place for potentially heated discussions is not during the ministry part of the trip, but rather during a designated time of debrief. If the team knows they will get an opportunity to air their concerns, have their pressing questions answered, or be able to resolve relational problems, then they will be able to focus on the ministry.

Of course, a daily team meeting for brief discussion is ideal. But any issues that are raised at the daily meeting that could cause division or distraction should be tabled until the scheduled, uninterrupted debrief. At this time each individual should have time alone with the team leader so that he or she can determine what needs to be dealt with privately between two members, and what the whole team needs to discuss together.

Some teams are so mature and compatible that the debrief is little more than a recap of how enjoyable and profitable the time has been. This shared report of what each person has learned, enjoyed, or experienced can be very edifying and should be fostered and facilitated by the team leader. But when unfinished business lurks in the background, the debrief is the time to bring it to the fore and deal with it.

The best time and place for a debrief session is after the final good-bye with the host church and missionary, away from the environment where the ministry has been done. This signals the closure of the ministry section and helps usher in the perspective that some of the issues were specific to the location and environment.

For example, one trip to Japan was taxing on my team's nerves because the humidity was oppressive; the food was . . . exotic (including raw eel, whale blubber, and fermented beans that would be considered hazardous waste back home); and the cultural atmosphere was one of high-paced productivity, incessant meetings, and not much sleep (and even that was done on the floor!). Every morning there was a meeting conducted in English, followed by a meeting conducted in Japanese to prepare for the ministry. After the ministry, there were meetings about the day's events, and other meetings about the next day's events.

Early mornings, very late nights, indigestion, and mild heatstroke made for some team members becoming cranky and short with one another and requesting to skip some of the increasingly redundant meetings in order to rest. The last thing the team needed was another meeting to discuss why we needed to meet! The debrief session had to be someplace fun and informal, like a beach in Hawaii, which just happened to be the one-day layover we had arranged. By the time that session was called, the tensions about the other meetings had evaporated. Sometimes just getting into a new location in the world makes a world of difference.

Here are topics the team leader should cover at the posttrip debrief:

- Any residual interpersonal issues that have not been handled privately
- Financial reconciliation of expenses, gathering of receipts, etc.
- Putting a person in charge of collecting and collating a disc of everyone's individual digital pictures (knowing that this will happen helps the team be more efficient with taking group pictures in-country; nobody wants to take the same picture with fourteen cameras, when you can take it once and share it with the whole team)
- Preparation on how to communicate the experience (as discussed later in this chapter)

- Setting a date for the STM report to the sending church (it is important for the whole team to be present for the public report)
- Schedule for thank-you letters to be sent to supporters
- Reminders to follow through on any commitments made to locals, including keeping in touch with the missionary family and others
- Suggested improvements for future trips
- Sharing some spiritual lessons each person learned
- Sharing other highlights of the trip
- Setting a date for a team reunion within a few weeks of returning

It may also be appropriate for the team to thank the team leader for the effort and leadership rendered by means of a gift or letter of thanks signed by the team. If there are any complaints about the team leader, that should be done privately and followed up with the church leadership at home.

ROUGH LANDING

For those who have not traveled across time zones before, the physical toll of an STM trip can be unexpectedly fatiguing. Usually the STMer has used their vacation leave from work or school in order to minister. The time they would normally use to recoup from a demanding workload or course load has been swallowed whole by the STM trip. The trip has by no means been relaxing, but your boss might expect you to perform like anyone else who just had three weeks off work, which is to say well rested and ready for action. In reality you need a vacation from your "vacation."

Another often unavoidable self-destructive scheduling maneuver is to return to work too soon after returning. To maximize your time on the mission field, you might neglect to designate some of your leave for downtime at home. If you have a choice, though, it is highly recommended to take a day or two to catch up on sleep (and laundry) as well as preparing yourself for the barrage of questions you will receive from people who inquire, "So, how was the trip?" with varying degrees of sincerity or feigned interest.

You will be battling insomnia and its resultant fatigue. Your muscle memory will continue to move your hands in gestures meant to assist understanding, leaving your speech patterns with a redundant overarticulation and flustered affectation. Sometimes you will still speak slower than you need to, either coming across as condescending to your peers, or leaving the impression you have suffered some sort of head trauma. So be aware that you are now home, and you don't need to make a pouring gesture when you ask a waitress to get you some water.

There may also be an unexpected emotional adjustment when you reenter your world. It is surprising how attached you can become to orphans whose names you only learned a few days before. Deep friendships can be forged with astonishing rapidity. These strangers you shook hands with at the airport arrivals three weeks before, you were weepily hugging like family at the departures area. Names you were trying to remember on day three are now etched in your memory forever. This is a common experience with ministering alongside like-minded believers with common goals, compassion, beliefs, and spiritual perspectives.

As you settle into your normal routine, the realization sets in that you may not see these friends ever again this side of eternity. And it's sad. You are haunted by the faces of these loved ones whose lives you touched and who left a lasting impression on your soul. This is not something you anticipated when you were planning the trip and looking forward to the experience. The dramatic experience has come and gone. But people around you don't seem to care that you just made and lost real friends. There isn't much you can do about this besides being aware that it's coming. Recognize that it's normal and healthy to grow so close to other believers in so short a time, and that it is perfectly normal to miss them. Many STMers end up returning many times to the same field because of this emotional attachment. And praise God for that. Others prefer to try new fields, to make even more friends, whom they will reunite with in heaven. But very few decide that the ecstasy of international ministry wasn't worth the agony that accompanies the experience. In fact, many who decide to become permanent missionaries do so because they get to make friends and never leave them.

Spiritually there will be a maturing that has lasting effects. You may experience a subtle or even dramatic shift in your worldview. Your view of poverty and wealth, family and career, eternal and temporal goals can send tremors of change in your world. Your priorities now have a foil to compare them to. You have managed to be happy and fulfilled in an environment that you had previous thought of as distasteful. You may even have realized that your way of living life—the goals you pursue, the friends you make, the food you eat—is inferior to that of the people you went to help. You now envy the people you previously pitied. It can be disconcerting to be faced with this existential crisis. Wisdom would dictate that you not make any dramatic decisions until you have been back for a month or two. This will tell you how much of your thinking is due to an actual spiritual maturing that will permanently move the rudder of your life to a new direction, and how much was merely emotional gusts of wind that made you temporarily lose your balance.

GUILT TRIP

Processing your experience and reentering your old, privileged life, may cause a "reverse culture shock." You may feel guilty about how little you do for the kingdom compared to the missionaries you met. Or your guilt may come from how much you own, compared with the starving orphans you ministered to.

This is a matter of conscience and maturity. It is a simple fact of life that some people are rich and others are poor. The fact that you had the choice and the resources to travel to a foreign country and back puts you squarely in the category of more privileged than most. Each Christian needs to determine before God what they are able and willing to sacrifice for the sake of others who are less physically well-off. But it is a misunderstanding to think that having resources at your disposal (i.e., being rich enough to meet your needs and more) is sin in itself. It is also far too convenient and simplistic to say that since having wealth is not sinful there is no need to consider sharing it with others. The important thing to remember when you return is that your emotions are raw and reeling; it is not a good time to make drastic decisions. Write down how you feel and what you want to do, and then make an appointment with yourself in six weeks to act on those decisions. This will give you time to think biblically, being convicted by the Spirit for your sin, but without the false guilt that you feel as a result of emotional confusion.

COMMUNICATING YOUR EXPERIENCE

Everyone will inquire how your trip was, but not everyone really cares. You need to be able to sift the wheat from the tares here. For the casual question, you need a pithy answer. Choose two words and a single sentence to meaningfully describe your trip that will have the effect of piquing further interest. This whiff from the nutshell might engender a follow-up question. For example, if you describe your trip as "emotionally moving," or "spiritually enlightening," or "personally convicting," or "devastatingly humbling," these intriguing descriptors engender the desire for elaboration. If the person responds with "In what way?" or "How so?" you can offer an intriguing sentence to further lure out those who were initially just being polite, but are now curious. You may explain, "Being deprived for three weeks of so much I take for granted, has really made me reconsider my priorities," or "Living with and ministering alongside believers whose worldview is so dissimilar to mine, but whose spiritual outlook is identical, really caused me to realize how culturally transcendent the gospel is."

These descriptions highlight your unique perspective and intimately personal experience, and not the typical shallow superficialities that most people spew out when asked about their travels. The purpose of talking about the trip is to share with others what God has shown you. If your first words are about the unhygienic toilets, gagging culinary disasters, and oppressive humidity, then you have dragged the sacred into the mundane. You have missed an opportunity to bring back with you the unique spiritual lessons that made your trip different from a tourist excursion. Rather than give your listener a predictable and banal earful of why "there's no place like home," seize the moment to minister to them with the realities that make STM trips otherworldly. Or as the Apostle Paul, the archetypal STMer, put it: "Set your minds on things that are above, not on things that are on earth" (Col 3:2).

TRAVEL PUFFS UP

Firsthand exposure to the world's diversity is one of the great personal benefits of STM. You return a different person, and hopefully more spiritually mature. You may have met people who are more needy than you and yet, mysteriously, more content than you. Perhaps you experienced spiritual lessons in dying to self, considering others more highly than yourself, and loving your neighbor as yourself. There is the benefit you glean of getting a glimpse into how global and transcultural God's work in the world is. You see the pettiness of your own preferences and personal peeves, and the blinkers of your cultural bias gets ripped off your eyes and replaced by a panorama of different ways to worship God. In short, you experience what feels like a spiritual upgrade.

And then you come back down from your spiritual cloud nine, back to earth with an anticlimactic thud. Your coworkers are still focused on the same trivialities that you were preoccupied with before you left—money, sports, fashion, status, and a plethora of other topics that you now deplore. This is a recipe for unspiritual attitudes that lead to unsocial behavior. Nobody enjoys being around a holier-than-thou know-it-all. If you mismanage your relationships back home, you could forfeit an opportunity to share what you learned with others.

The problem is that "'knowledge' puffs up" (1 Cor 8:1). You learn so much about yourself and about God and about the ministry that you can't remember a time that you didn't know these truths. But for everyone back home, they remember you being that way all too well. After all, it's only been three weeks. It helps to remember that anything you have been given is a gift from God, which should be received humbly and used for his glory. As Paul warned the Corinthians who were boasting in their newfound spiritual enlightenment, "For who sees anything different in you? What do you have that you did not receive? If then you received it, why do you boast as if you did not receive it?" (1 Cor 4:7).

EXPERT SYNDROME

Closely related to the spiritual pride that comes from traveling is the concomitant temptation to view oneself as well versed in all things pertaining to life abroad. Many travelers who avoided catching a physically debilitating illness, return in full health, only to succumb to a much more insidious malady—"expert syndrome."

Frank Abagnale was notorious for his ability to fake expertise in professional fields as diverse as law and medicine. Throughout the 1960s, Abagnale duped dozens of colleagues into accepting him as a peer in fields that required high levels of expertise. He faked careers as a doctor, lawyer, law enforcement officer, teacher, and most astonishingly as an airline pilot. He tried cases, supervised medical procedures, taught sociology classes, and flew passenger planes, all before his twenty-first birthday. The secret of his seemingly prodigious abilities was to confidently play the part. No one dared question his apparent expertise.

When travelers return from STM trips, it is expected that they regale their friends and family with dazzling tales of their intrepid globe-trotting. In those moments, their listeners may begin to ask questions about the country's history, politics, culture, and geography. It may be tempting to respond with authoritative pontification with unfounded confidence.

Your fortnight of experience does not make you an automatic expert on a country, nor on missions in general. It is disingenuous to opine about this or that topic as if you were a pundit.

I spent a few days in Calcutta and Mumbai on a leg of an STM trip. Naturally I was exposed to those in dire circumstances. If I had been asked if India was one of the fastest growing economies in the world, boasting a considerably robust number of PhD graduates, software tycoons, millionaires, and people with aristocratic lifestyles, I would have flatly denied it. But my perception of India was based on a few selective slices of experience limited by my purpose for being in the country—missionaries tend not to live in the millionaires' neighborhoods. If I had come as a tourist, or a businessman, or a student, my experience would have been vastly different. On the flight home I watched a documentary highlighting the astonishing diversity of Indian culture, economics, society, religion, and lifestyles. I'm thankful for that reminder that I was practically ignorant of most of the country I was about to report on. That realization helped me limit my presentation to phrases that showed how unrepresentative my experience was. I used phrases like, "in the part of the city where we ministered, this was my impression . . .; in the area we visited, among the people we spoke to, their lives seemed to be . . ."

Playing the know-it-all is annoying enough, but when the proffered information is riddled with inaccuracies, the report is unhelpful, and also unworthy of those involved in Christian missions. A strong blend of humility and honesty is the best antidote to the deplorable disease of "expert syndrome."

FOLLOW-THROUGH

Everybody knows that a trip to the grocery store is not complete when you've arrived back at home, but only when the groceries are carried in and packed away. In the same way, the purpose of the STM trip is not considered to be accomplished by a safe touchdown back home. The final stage of ministry must include the follow-through of reporting to the sending church, thanking donors, and establishing communication with the missionaries.

Reporting to the Sending Church

As we learned in previous chapters about the main target of a missions trip, the bull's eye of purpose for the STM trip is the missionary family. But although your sending church is not the primary impact zone, it is still one of the important factors that make STM trips profitable. There are many benefits for your local church that come from sending a team to their missionaries. First, it fosters a necessary, supportive, and personal relationship with the missionaries by sending members to fellowship with them. Second, it infuses the sending church with zeal and excitement for missions by providing for a tangible way to serve the missionaries. Third, the trip will undoubtedly help mature the individuals who travel, thus blessing the whole congregation indirectly with men and women who are more eager to be involved and more equipped to do so. And fourth, the eyewitness report of information gained about the missionaries' ministry helps the congregation to be more involved in the lives of the missionaries.

It is important to rekindle the memory of those in the pit. It is far too easy to be part of a decision to support a ministry while at the church's annual general meeting, and then to forget about the missionaries until the following year's ministry review. Photographs of the environment in which the ministry functions can bring an abstract report to life. The congregation needs to see in living color that their missionaries are more than just a line item on the church budget; they are a family who live and laugh and sweat and serve in a real place that has real challenges and real needs.

Hearing reports from people who were so recently present with the missionaries, helps the congregation to pray more effectively and may nudge some of them to contact the missionaries themselves. Also, hearing reports of how the financial contribution of a church is bearing fruit in foreign fields assists the church in being wise stewards of their money and may spur them on to contribute more significantly in the future.

Many churches allow the STM team a slot in the main Sunday service to report back: an extended announcement time, or perhaps an entire service of testimonies. Other churches opt to have a distinct "missions report night" at a dedicated time in the week. Either way, the report should be done shortly after the return, so that the congregation is not hearing in the official report the same as what they have already heard one-on-one from the STMers. The fresh news should come hot off the presses.

The report should include information about the ministry's location, objectives, and *modus operandi*. Rather than merely statistical, objective information, there can also be testimonies about some local individuals who have been effected by the ministry. Special attention can be given to the missionary family, including their particular challenges, so that prayer requests are suggested. The content should be fleshed out with testimonies by individuals on the team of how the trip impacted them, and the team leader could even suggest tangible ways congregants could get involved in the ministry. The stage is now also set for future trips. This public report should focus on the positive aspects; it should be inspiring and informative.

Thanking Donors

Mature believers who contribute financially to STM trips do not do it in order to be profusely thanked. But it is common courtesy to acknowledge the role anyone played in helping you go on the trip. Anyone who committed to help you—whether through prayer, rides to the airport, or financial donations—should be considered to have been your partner in this mission. They will receive eternal reward for their part, and you can increase their joy in missions by acknowledging their partnership.

A simple thank-you note may suffice, but you might also feel that it is appropriate to give them a meaningful memento of the trip (why else did God create keychains?). This shows that you remembered them and their role while you were abroad, and shows thoughtfulness. The exercise is, in a sense, also for your benefit—you need to be reminded that you were able to go because of God's grace as channeled through the generosity of his saints.

Establishing Communications with the Missionaries

Hopefully you do not view the missionaries as your personal tour guides, but rather as friends and partners in the mission to bring Jesus global glory. Friendships forged on the field with locals, fellow teammates, and the missionary family, are all rewarding aspects of STM ministry. Establishing a "pen-pal" type email relationship is very helpful for the missionary family. They are the ones who stayed behind with the difficulties and isolation while you returned to your comfort zone.

Foreign missions is lonely labor. It helps missionaries to know you remember them and care for them. An occasional email is all it takes, and this should be seen as part of the follow-through of your ministry. At the very least a single contact shortly after your return, expressing gratitude for their hosting, is in order. Just ask yourself what you would appreciate if you were the missionary and they were the visiting team (Matt 7:12).

CONCLUSION

William Booth, a preacher not known for mincing words, charged his congregation with an unambiguous challenge:

> "Not called!" did you say? "Not heard the call," I think you should say. Put your ear down to the Bible, and hear Him bid you go and pull sinners out of the fire of sin. Put your ear down to the burdened, agonized heart of humanity, and listen to its pitiful wail for help. Go stand by the gates of hell, and hear the damned entreat you to go to their father's house and bid their brothers and sisters and servants and masters not to come there. Then look Christ in the face—whose mercy you have professed to obey—and tell Him whether you will join heart and soul and body and circumstances in the march to publish His mercy to the world.[13]

Every faithful believer must be part of God's plan; he or she must respond to Christ's commission to take the good news of salvation to all the nations. Participating in or supporting STM trips is a tangible way missions-minded believers can undergird the evangelization of the world. Not everyone can board a plane, nor should they need to. But everyone must play their position in this orchestrated campaign.

Holding the ropes is no less vital to the success of the mission than it is to penetrate the dark pit. Short-term missions is a simple and effective way in

---

13 Quoted in Edward Deritany, *When God Calls You* (Nashville: Thomas Nelson, 1976), 76.

which the local church can actively involve themselves in the lives and work and ministries of the missionaries whom God has called to serve away from the comforts, conveniences, safety, and familiarity of home.

It is my hope and prayer for you that you are moved to participate in the duty and delight of missions—either by considering pursuing the thrilling and rewarding adventure of long-term, lifetime missions, or by supporting those who do, financially, as well as through short-term missions. Not everyone can go into the pit, but all Christians can take their stand, grasp the support line, and join the ranks of those faithfully holding the ropes.

BIBLIOGRAPHY

Archer, Clint. "Short-term Missions: Supporting and Directing Those We Send." In *Rediscovering Biblical Evangelism*, edited by John MacArthur, 293–305. Nashville: Thomas Nelson, 2011.

Belcher, John. *William Carey: A Biography*. Philadelphia: American Baptist Publication Society, 1853.

Bryson, Bill. *At Home*. London: Transworld, 2010.

Carey, Eustace. *Memoir of William Carey, D. D.* London: Jackson & Walford, 1836.

Carey, S. Pearce. *William Carey*. London: Wakeman Trust, 1993.

Deritany, Edward. *When God Calls You*. Nashville: Thomas Nelson, 1976.

Spurgeon, Charles. "The Wailing of Risca." A sermon delivered at Exeter Hall, London, December 9, 1860. Print version found in *The Metropolitan Pulpit, Vol. 7*, sermon 349.

INDEX